"I now make contacts everywhere I go. If I have 30 seconds to spare, I know how to use it to meet people, qualify them and sometimes even walk away with a sale."

Gloria Gault Geary
Speaker, Author and Spokesperson

"If you are just starting out and could buy only one book to help you succeed, this is the book."

Tom Delehanty
Hughes Television Network & Professional Actor

"As a result of this book, I've made more business and personal contacts in the last 60 days than I have in the last 5 years."

Mark Elia, President
Mark of Excellence Home Remodeling

"I've used the information in the book and the authors' services and my career skyrocketed."

Steven Gaffney
Professional Speaker & President of POWER

"Great advice from two guys who know what it takes to build a reputation while growing a business. You'll do well to have these two as your mentors by reading this idea-filled book."

Dave Voracek
Founder, The Marketing Department

"Read the book, practice the concepts, sign-up the customers — you can't lose!"

Michael P. O'Brien
Insurance Agent & Field Underwriter

"The book has opened up even more doors for me."

William H. Bruce, P.h.D.
Author, How I Became a Millionaire Buying, Renting & Selling Real Estate

"I've tripled my prospects and doubled my customers and it's only Tuesday!"

Bill Vesey
President, Vesey Business Consultants

NOBODY to SOMEBODY
in 63 Days or Less

**The Ultimate How-To Guide To
Business
Networking
&
Word of Mouth
Advertising**

Joseph C. Ilvento   Arnold Sanow

Published by
Applied Business Communications, Inc.
United States of America

Applied Business Communications, Inc.
P.O. Box 2583
Woodbridge, Virginia 22193

3 5 7 9 10 8 6 4 2

Library of Congress Cataloging-in-Publication Data
Ilvento, Joseph C. & Sanow, Arnold
Nobody to Somebody in 63 Days or Less
Joseph C. Ilvento & Arnold Sanow

ISBN 0-9654362-0-9

This book is dedicated to every person we have had the opportunity to meet, greet, trade and aid. With each and every encounter we honed and polished our networking skills. We especially want to thank those people, you know who you are, who wake up faithfully at 5 AM to make those early breakfast meetings, drive across town to make each business luncheon and miss dinner to attend every after hours reception.

Nobody to Somebody in 63 Days or Less

Preface

Becoming *someone* in life is an ambition most successful people have as a child and carry with them throughout their lives. Let's face it, most of us in this world were not born into a life of fame and fortune. If we want to make it in this world it is up to us and what we do today and tomorrow to make that dream a reality. This book was written as a catalyst to make the process of becoming a *somebody* quicker and easier. And we do mean quick — 63 days or less.

Think about it, there are some people who have been doing business in your community for more than 20 plus years and yet you have never heard of them. Is it that they really want to keep their business a secret? Is it that they have all the customers they need? What have they been doing for 20 years? This book will show you step-by-step, strategy-by-strategy how to become known throughout your community in a matter of weeks.

How do we know it will work? We've done it and have been doing it for years. And, we've been teaching others how to do it too. It's not hard and once you experience your first success, the rest is easy. Why? Because you too will find it is the easiest and most cost effective way to gain new contacts and customers that will transform your career and life!

The desire to make a name for yourself, to be a *somebody*, for some starts early in life, perhaps as early as grammar or high school. For many, it may come after college or within a few years of entering the workforce. And for others, it may happen much later later in life, possibly as the result of corporate downsizing, a divorce or career change. Regardless, the sooner you get to know the "right" people and the sooner the "right" people get to know you — the sooner your success in life — as you too become a *"somebody"* in a position to help others.

Unfortunately, many never seem to meet the "right" people. They say they are never in the *right* place at the *right* time. This book will change all that. Not only will you know how and where to meet the *"right"* people, but you will also know what to do with them once you meet them. Over time, you will meet so many *right* people and so many right people will know you that you will become one of those right people — a *somebody*. And as you may already know, life is much easier as a *somebody* than a nobody. The choice is yours.

Why 63 days? They say it takes 21 days to learn a new habit. We want you to get into the habit of networking. During your first 21-day cycle pick 5 to 10 basic networking concepts and practice them every chance you get. During the second 21-day cycle, perfect your basic skills and layer another 10 to 15 skills as needed. Finally, during the third 21-day cycle, practice the basics and apply any and all strategies as needed. Have fun!

A Note to the Reader

This book is designed as a handbook of sorts to be used in whole or in part depending on the specific needs of the reader. To expedite your success in benefiting from the concepts and strategies put forward, we have organized the book into three major sections. The first section deals with strategies you should employ *before* the networking opportunity, the second section on strategies you can employ *during* the networking opportunity and yes, you guessed it, the third section focuses on strategies you can employ *after* the event.

Although you can turn to any page in this book and benefit immediately from the strategy or technique offered, you will find that a synergy exists when the strategies are used in conjunction with one another. When the strategies are combined, what results is a exponential effect that will "wow" those you meet for the first time. It is the power of this initial first impression coupled with proven follow-up strategies that will begin the transformation of turning you from a so-called *nobody* into a *somebody* in 63 days or less.

We suggest that you read the book cover to cover, take notes in the margin and earmark those pages you can apply immediately to your unique personal and professional environment. Some of the techniques are "must do" such as name badges, 30/60 second commercials, lead leveraging, and membership in various organizations. Other techniques, such as arriving early, staying late and volunteer work are not critical, but will greatly reduce the amount of time it takes to become a somebody. Regardless of which tools you use, note your results and stick with those that bring you the greatest success. Most of all, have fun. We looking forward to meeting *you* someday.

About the Authors

Joseph C. Ilvento has been labeled by those who know him as the "King of Networking." He has used the ideas and concepts found in this book for years and shares them with audiences around the world. He practices what he preaches. Every day he can be found either giving or getting business leads solely on the basis of the networking techniques found in this book.

He is the best "how to" speaker on business networking and word-of-mouth advertising strategies. He is a pro at teaching others how to walk into a crowded room of strangers and walk out with hot sales leads and business. As Publisher of *Market Monthly Magazine* (visit the site on the world wide web at marketmonthly.com), he interacts with some of the best sales, marketing and management experts in the world today. If you want a *been there and done it* sales and marketing speaker at your next event, Joe Ilvento can be reached at 800-382-6343.

Arnold Sanow is known as "America's Marketing Strategist." He is the co-author of three books including the bestseller, *Marketing Boot Camp*. He works with clients throughout the world to develop their marketing plans and strategies. He has delivered over 2,000 presentations for small and large businesses, associations and government organizations. He is a frequent guest on radio, television and in the print media.

Recent appearances include the *Wall Street Journal, CBS Evening News with Dan Rather, USA Today, Entrepreneur Magazine* and others. He has been a national spokesperson for companies such as AT&T and Intuit. In addition, he is an adjunct professor at Georgetown University in Washington, D.C. If you need a marketing or communications speaker or trainer, spokesperson, writer or business or marketing strategist, you can reach Arnold Sanow at 703-255-3133 or 800-584-7382.

Section One:
Strategies to Employ Prior to The Networking Event

Section Two:
Strategies to Employ During the Networking Event

Section Three:
Strategies to Employ After the Networking Event

As marketing consultants who teach people the importance of marketing themselves and their businesses, we have the unique opportunity to see what works and what doesn't. One of the key strategies we encourage people to use is word of mouth advertising. It is the available marketing weapon all businesses possess and, as you will see in this book, when honed and polished can become one of your most cost effective and efficient tools.

Getting other people to tout the benefits of you and your business is a learned skill possessed by true marketing experts. Chapter after chapter, this book will show you how to integrate your marketing efforts to achieve maximum word of mouth exposure. Business cards, advertising, internet exposure and even your name badge all contribute to one's word of mouth advertising formula.

If you are like most people we know, odds are you have to contend with an ever increasing array of competitors. Each one undercutting the other's price while simultaneously offering more benefits leaving fewer and fewer profits on the table. One way to become, and remain, profitable is to work smarter (and harder) than the other *guy*.

Your mission is to develop marketing and sales methods whereby you obtain customers and contacts at a far lower cost than that of your competitors. If your competitor runs an ad in the local paper at a cost of $1,000 that results in four new customers, you might say his acquisition cost per new customer was $250.

What if you were able to obtain those same four customers at a cost of only $5 per customer? I think you would agree with us, that possessing such a powerful advantage over your competitors would be to your benefit. This book shows you how to gain such a strategic advantage in literally 63 days or less. Chapter after chapter, technique after technique you will learn how to layer and position each strategy to gain customers at little or no out-of-pocket cost.

If you don't market or make yourself known to your potential customers, you might as well be a *nobody*. Creating a reputation that precedes you is what effective advertising and marketing is all about. For example, everyday people buy new products and services based, in part, on the ads they saw on television or in print. Think of the ad as the handshake, the first impression, the introduction. And in real life, if the handshake is firm, the first impression strong, and the introduction interesting — you are on your way to gaining a new customer.

If you don't have the luxury of television advertising working for you or for that matter even a local print ad, YOU become the message. How YOU shake hands matters. How YOU introduce yourself to others and describe what you do matters. How YOU are perceived by others is up to YOU. Why not capitalize on each and every opportunity available to you when meeting someone for the first time? Why not do your best to make a perfect and memorable first impression and gain a customer for life? The choice is yours and the chapters that follow will show you how easy it can be to become a *Somebody*.

Whether you want to triple the number of customers you obtain as a result of word of mouth advertising or just increase your strategic influence with those you already know, this book is a must read. We're confident you will find this book a great addition to your personal and professional library.

▲

Before we jump into the invaluable concepts and strategies found in this book, we must first define the concept of networking. Generally speaking, the concept of networking in a business context should be viewed as any opportunity to meet or come in contact with, either directly or indirectly, anyone who can further your personal or professional goals and objectives. The more people you know who can help you further your goals and objectives, the easier those goals and objectives become to achieve. *Each and every person, and we mean everyone, you come in contact with should be treated as a networking opportunity.*

There are two key learning points in that last sentence that are critical to possessing the right attitude towards becoming a professional networker. The first is that everyone you meet should be treated as a potential customer — even the unruly looking gas station attendant with dirty finger nails. The fact that most people see right through these kinds of people, as you will learn from this book, is to your advantage. Although this particular individual may not become your biggest customer, his uncle or brother or best friend's mother may.

One basic rule to successful networking is the more people you know — or better yet, the more people who know of you — the more business you will earn as a result of word of mouth advertising. Let's assume the average person knows 250 people on a personal basis. If you work alone and have not used your networking skills up to this point, your prospect database is limited to the people you know, the cold calls you make and any advertising that generates new contacts. However, if you tap into this networking potential, in addition to your own contacts, cold calls and advertising leads, you also tap into the *sphere of influence* of those around you. If we again assume that each person has 250 personal contacts in his or her personal network, networking with one person increases your contact base by 250. Networking with 10 people increases your contact base by 2,500 and networking with 100 people, increases your network base by 25,000. Over time, it is not uncommon for professional networkers to increase their personal contact base to over 1,000 people, thus increasing your networking base to over 250,000.

As you increase your contact base great things begin to happen. The phone rings more. The cash register rings more and eventually you can operate in a 100% referral environment. Can you imagine never again having to spend time or money on traditional advertising? Think about how many times you hear people talking about an upcoming purchase, improvement, sale, move, invest- ment, etc. However, you know you will capitalize on what you overhear, the key to networking success is to get your contact base of 250 or 2,500 or 25,000 to recog- nize and forward the information to you.

People like to refer their friends and family to others who can help them. Professional networkers have trained, yes trained, their contact base how to recognize a need for their product or service. For example, a telecommunications representative turns rotary phones into money. He pays $100 for each one on a trade-in basis. His network knows to call him when they learn about a person who uses a rotary phone. A life insurance saleswoman trains her contact base that when they see a pregnant woman, especially for the first time, to also see a life insurance policy. She now receives calls every week with "pregnant women sightings" and she writes more life insurance than anyone in her office.

When you have a sales team of 25,000 out there on the street looking for opportunities on your behalf, business is soon to follow. Sometimes, the opportunities are very obvious. People may come right out and ask your contact base if they know a good stock broker, or accountant or insurance agent. At a minimum, your contact base should hit networking opportunities like this out of the park. Instantly, your name and ideally your phone number should come to mind. The best way to do this is to keep your name and number in front of your contact base.

The second key learning point is the use of the word *opportunity* to describe every interaction you and your contact base has with others. When you fill your car with gas and pay the attendant, an *opportunity* exists to make yourself known to that person. You can be overt and introduce yourself outright or indirectly through the use of an interesting name tag or outfit. *Do you currently take advantage of opportunities like this?* Remember, the intent of this approach is not to sell the gas attendant, but to sell everyone he or she knows. The fact remains an *opportunity* to expand your contact base by 250 exists and it doesn't cost you anything. Think about it, each day you have the *opportunity* to increase your contact base by 250, 1,000, even 10,000!

Think of your contact base as a huge direct mail program. Depending on your audience and subject matter, most experts will agree that a two percent or less response rate on your mailing is about average. The same holds true with your networking contact base. So if you have a solid, trained networking base of 1,000 people it is not unrealistic to expect 20 new customers a year as a result of referrals and word of mouth advertising. Remember, we said a solid, well trained contact base. That's a contact base of people who refer your name and number without hesitation. Although you may now only have a solid contact base of 10, with the help of this book, it will begin to grow day after day, week after week and it soon will be in the hundreds or thousands.

Networking opportunities often will occur in one on one situations but, as you will learn, there are various events designed to maximize your exposure to others. For the purpose of this book, we will cover all staged events such as Chamber of Commerce events (to include all Civic clubs, etc.), Lead Groups (to include exclusive and non-exclusive groups) and general receptions (to include both business and private functions such as weddings, parties, bars) and also show you how to create your own event.

Regardless of where the event takes place, if you are prepared and know how to capitalize on every 30 second opportunity you have available to you when meeting others, the results can be dramatic. So dramatic people will want to know how you do it. So dramatic people will talk about you. So dramatic people will label you with a reputation as "the best" in your industry. You will become a *Somebody*.

Section

Strategies to Employ PRIOR to the Networking Event

The Old Alarm Clock

First things first. Many of the events you will be attending are early 7 AM breakfast meetings. Some will be in your neighborhood, but to fully capitalize on all of the networking opportunities available to you in your immediate area, you must be prepared to do what it takes to make the event. Professional networkers will not think twice about driving an hour to make an event. Consequently, one of the most critical "do whatever it takes to succeed" traits is your ability to wake up in the morning. Pretty basic stuff, right? Wrong. Not wanting or having the ability to wake up early is the primary reason people give us as to why they don't attend these early morning functions. Now, if you are a morning person you shouldn't have a problem with this basic concept. However, if you are like most of America and don't particularly relish getting up at 5 AM, you may need a little help.

It is not uncommon for many networking breakfasts to begin at 7 AM. Consequently, when you factor in the time it takes to shower, get dressed, gather your materials and get out the door, for most of us that means getting up no later than 6 AM. Now factor in drive time, traffic delays, bad weather, arriving 15 minutes early, parking, and anything unexpected — now you are looking at a "wake-up and rise time" of 5 AM.

So how do you ensure that you will have the ability to get your tired bones out of bed? First, make sure you have a reliable alarm clock. If you are serious about networking, you'll invest in an alarm clock with a battery back-up to eliminate power outage excuses and a double alarm setting to override the snooze button.

But there is more. Now that you have your alarm clock double set and ready to go, we suggest setting the two alarms in 5 minute intervals, i.e., 5:00 AM and 5:05 AM. But wait, there is still more. Now, place the armed clock in the bathroom — preferably close to the shower. Make sure the alarm volume knob is turned up high enough to hear from your bedroom (test it) and there is nothing you will trip over on the floor from your bed to the alarm clock. Remember, if you are not used to getting up early, you're operating on "radar" for the first five or ten minutes.

Sound excessive? But if the event you are attending is held only once a year, missing it or arriving late could mean the difference between success and failure. Following this advice will allow for "no excuses" as to why you did not make the meeting that could have introduced you to the person who was waiting to hand you the biggest sale you ever had.

Night Before Preparation

In addition to setting your alarm clock, also take a few minutes the night before and layout the clothes, under-garments, socks, stockings, shoes, and anything else you need to get ready in the morning. If you are a coffee lover and have a coffee pot with a timer on it, believe me, there is nothing better in the early hours of the morning than to have a hot cup of coffee waiting for you when you wake up. Depending on how much of a morning motivator a cup of "Joe" is to you, you may want to move the coffee pot into the bathroom and place it right next to your alarm clock.

For those of you who are not early risers, unless you are a news hound, let us assure you that at 5 AM there is not much on the radio. You may want to pick out a few lively audio tapes and sing yourself into an upbeat frenzy ready to take on the networking opportunities that await you. Don't let anything slow you down. Gather all your business tools and have them ready by the door or better yet, in your car. Things to include: a full supply of business cards, a calculator, a pen, a sales agreement (hey, you never know), a few breath mints, and anything else you might use or need during your meeting.

Again, you don't want anything to get between you and your meeting, especially a gas station. Make sure you are gassed up and ready to go. Back your car into the driveway so all you need to do is get into your car, put it in drive and put the pedal to the metal. If you don't have a travel-type coffee mug, get one — a big one. It eliminates the need to stop off and pick up a cup of coffee on the way. If you live in an area where snow and ice are factors, make sure you leave enough time for your car to warm up and windows to defrost. Although your mechanic may not agree, start your car and get the heater going up to 15 minutes before you expect to leave. There is nothing worse than doing everything it takes to get up early only to have to sit in a freezing car with iced over windows for 20 minutes waiting for it to warm up.

En Route

Depending on where you live and the traffic patterns of the morning or afternoon rush hours, knowing a few alternate routes to where you are going can mean the difference in getting there and getting there on time. If you are planning on an early morning commute, after turning your alarm off, check the local radio stations for a rush hour traffic report. For example, in the Washington, D.C. area, a single accident on one of the major traffic arteries can mean upwards of an hour delay in traffic if an alternative route is not scheduled early in the commute.

Knowing the back roads, as well as the exact address and exact location of the event can save hours of time and aggravation. At the time that you learn of the event, take a moment to jot down specific directions on how to get there. Also, ask about the best place to park, area garages that offer discounts, and the exact name and phone number of the restaurant or location where you plan to meet.

A cellular phone comes in very handy when you get caught in traffic or just can't seem to find the event. If you don't have a cellular, do not hesitate to pull over and use a pay phone or stop and ask for directions. If you are really lost, many area convenience stores will carry local street maps.

If you don't already have a detailed, local street map of the area, invest in one. Contact your local real estate agent and ask if they have an old one they would give or sell you. Real estate maps often combine multiple counties or towns into a single, large format map and are far less expensive than if you had to buy each map independently. Even though a good map may cost you $25 or more, it will more than pay for itself the next time you get caught in traffic. While everyone else is stuck on the major roads, you will have information at your fingertips to access the back roads and arrive at your destination with little or no loss of time.

Confirm Time, Date and Place

A professional networker is a good time manager. Prior to investing the time and effort into getting where you need to go, your first step is to confirm the time, date and location of the event. On average, probably ten percent of the 50+ networking events you will attend over the year, will be cancelled, postponed, relocated or be misprinted. If you live in an area where weather is a factor, confirm what the cancellation policy is in the event of snow. Is the meeting tagged to a local school closing, government closing, or delayed opening policy? After all, why should you go out in bad weather only to arrive and find the meeting has been cancelled.

Taking the time to confirm time, date and place details does two things. First, it ensures the time you invest in preparing for the meeting is not wasted. Remember, if you waste a couple of hours of your valuable time attending a non-event, that is a couple of hours that could have been invested into another event across town. And second, you have an opportunity to contact the organizer or a key contact person prior to attending the event. Showing up at an event where you are a complete stranger can be rather intimidating at first. However, having talked by phone to the group president or staff member, you have a name to start with. Ask if they will be at the meeting, and let them know you look forward to meeting them. Note their names and look for them around the check-in table at the event. Again, reintroduce yourself. Make them your first contact of the day. Let them know what you do and have them introduce you to the president. There are people we know who have been members of the local Chamber of Commerce for 10 years and have yet to meet the president — just think you've been there 10 minutes and you already know this person on a first name basis.

You may also want to use the time to review who else will be attending the event. Not that you would recognize names, but ask for the company names or personal titles of those attending. This will help you prepare and make your networking efforts easier.

Arrive Early

One of the best ways to ensure that you meet the movers and shakers of an event is to arrive early. We suggest at least 15 minutes, however, depending on the event, you may want to arrive upwards of one hour in advance.

It is typically the event planners, the guest speakers and the president of the organization who arrive very early to an event. If these are the kinds of people you want to meet, go early to the event. Take this time to briefly introduce yourself and ask if you can help setting up. Often, organizers don't have everything under control and the offer to lend a helping hand can be rewarding, especially if someone is late or does not show up. Areas where you may be of help include the moving and setting up of tables and chairs, the placement of signs on entrance doors and in lobby areas, the distribution of event materials, or the adjustment of heat or air conditioning.

Also, by being the first one there you will have the opportunity to capture and meet each person who arrives at the event one by one. Stand near the entrance of the event area. After people sign in and put on a name badge, take the time to casually introduce yourself and get the person's business card. The amount of time you spend with each person should be in direct proportion to the flow at which new people are arriving.

So, if a new person is arriving approximately every minute, spend no more than a minute with each person so you can maximize your introduction and exposure with each new attendee. Make a mental note of the people you cannot personally greet as they come in the door. This approach will ensure that you take full advantage of the event.

At a minimum, if you helped set up, you will be remembered by the staff. Feel free to ask them to introduce you to any key prospects you may have inadvertently overlooked.

Attendance

Regularly attending the functions and meetings of the groups where you have opted to become a member is critical. Referral networking is most successful when the people in the group know and trust you. A big part of building trust comes in the form of your reputation. People will form an impression about you based on your actions; attendance is one of the first actions you broadcast to others. Are you reliable and dependable? Are you on time? Are you early? Do you show up prepared to do business?

The answers to these questions say a lot about who you are and form the foundation of how existing group members (your prospects) will think about you. If members of the group feel you are dependable and can rely on your attendance, they are more likely to invite prospects to the event for you to meet. However, the opposite is also true. If you have a spotty attendance record, rarely will others in the group invite guests to attend to meet you; doing so will only make them look bad if you are not there.

Another tip with regards to attendance is to schedule and attend one-time or critical events. We suggest that you work backwards and develop your networking schedule accordingly. Identify those important events that are only held once a year and mark them in your calendar. Then identify and mark those events that are only held twice a year or quarterly. Then mark events with that are held monthly, and finally, schedule in your weekly meetings.

Certain events, such as business trade shows and special networking opportunities should not be missed at any cost. Often the contacts generated from one important event can equal those generated in three months worth of smaller weekly events. Attendance is a critical component of professional networking. Being in the right place at the right time, to some may seem like luck, but to the professional networker, it is a calculated and planned event.

As a matter of fact, membership is not always a good thing. We suggest attending an organization's functions as a guest as often as possible prior to joining. As a member, attendance is expected. However, as a guest or prospective member, your attendance — even spotty attendance — is viewed as interest. Only join those groups whose meetings you will be able to regularly attend. Otherwise, membership could actually hurt, rather than help you.

Back-to-Back Appointments

One technique we suggest to ensure you get out the door is to schedule back-to-back appointments in the area where the networking event is to be held. If the event starts at 7 AM and is over at 8:30 AM, do your best to pre-arrange 9 AM appointments with clients or prospects in the immediate area. If appropriate, you may want to invite your client or prospect to the event itself and then continue your meeting after the event. This approach gives you multiple reasons to get out the door on time.

Also, take advantage of those meetings that are held across town or in areas where you have few customers. Did you ever hear a salesperson say, *"I am going to be in your neighborhood, and I thought I'd drop by....?"* There is a reason why salespeople use this line. It works. If you are indeed going to be in an area you normally don't frequent, use the event as an opportunity to do a little prospecting.

We suggest you comb through your Rolodex or company's customer files and look for prospects that have offices located in the area. Use the meeting as the basis for your call. You might call, introduce yourself and invite the prospect to the meeting. If the prospect agrees, you not only have a sales call, but you will know someone at the event and will arrive bearing guests. These are key traits of a professional networker. If the prospect says no and can't attend the function, ask if you can stop by before or after the event. More often than not, you will get a yes.

We suggest you collect business cards from those people you think would be potential customers for the prospect you plan to meet. Don't make a big deal about it, but when you arrive say something like, *"To bad you couldn't make the networking event. I hope you don't mind, but I collected the cards of a few people who might be potential customers for you.*" Hand the prospect the stack of business cards and casually move on with your business. If the prospect is a savvy business person, what you placed in his or her hand is more valuable than any complimentary pen could ever be.

One last technique to maximize your networking calendar is to clover leaf your appointments. The effective management of your time is critical if you want to become a professional networker. Think of your day to day sales appointments as a function of your networking appointments. The two should become interrelated, otherwise you will begin to view your networking events as an obstacle to making your sales appointments on time.

As you set your appointments for the day, week or month, be sure to look at your calendar and integrate them with your networking events. If you are going to be across town for a lunch meeting, don't schedule a sales appointment back at the office right after lunch. If you have to make an appointment with a customer, look at your calendar and see which networking event will bring you to that area. Schedule the appointment for that day, ideally just before or after the event. Better yet, invite your prospect to the event.

The deliberate integration of appointments with networking events will give you the time and energy you need to attend almost every networking event available to you. It is a simple, yet powerful strategy that you will soon find you cannot live without.

Cash, Credit Cards and Quarters

Don't you hate it when you are late for an event and you finally find a parking spot only to realize that you do not have any loose change to put into the parking meter? As a professional networker you should always keep some spare cash and coins hidden in your car. You never know when a networking event may pop up unexpectedly and it can be embarrassing if you don't have cash on hand to pay for the drink you just ordered or the breakfast you thought was complimentary.

When it comes to parking, keep a roll of quarters in your glove compartment or better yet in your trunk, so they are not handy to spend at the drive-through window. How many times have you parked, only to find the meter only takes quarters and will not accept your two dimes and a nickel. Worse yet, you have no change, only bills and there isn't a store nearby to get change.

In addition to change, it is also a good idea to keep a spare $20 hidden somewhere in your car. Not only is it handy in the event of small car emergencies, should you need money at the last minute, you know cash is only as far away as your car. As you will soon learn, when you leave your home at the last minute to attend an event there will be times when you leave your wallet or purse behind and that spare $20 will be your saving grace.

Finally, keep a spare credit card hidden somewhere in your car too. If you ask, your credit card company will provide you with a copy of your card for such occasions. Having an extra card comes in handy for major car problems, a tow, a tank of gas and of course, an unexpected client lunch. Remember, impressions are everything when it comes to networking and the last thing you want to be known as is the stock broker with no money or the life insurance agent who takes his client to McDonalds. There will be times when the $10 in your pocket will not cover the impromptu lunch for the $1 million prospect you met at your morning networking event.

Another money related item you should keep handy is a location directory of automatic teller machines for your particular bank. Again, when you are across town and need money fast, the directory will be a handy tool. You may also want to keep two directories: one for your bank and one for another popular bank in the region.

The last item you should keep on you is a telephone company credit card. If you don't have a portable phone and must make a call from the road, a calling card comes in very handy. Either request one from your existing long distance company or purchase a prepaid card from your neighborhood convenience store.

Car Etiquette

They say you can tell a lot about a person by the car they drive. Are you the kind of person whose five-year-old car looks like it just drove off the show room floor? If you are, congratulations! We envy your ability to keep your car spotless inside and out. However, if you are like most of us, it's probably a challenge to keep your car looking its best.

Remember the old saying, "You never get a second chance to make a good first impression?" Unfortunately, even if you do make a good first impression, it can be destroyed if the prospect sees you drive away in your banged-up, '74 Dodge Dart. Little does General Motors know, you have been using air bags since 1971 that is if you define air bags as 100 or so empty McDonalds, Burger King and Taco Bell bags that are strategically located around your car. On top of that add a child seat, a dirty ash tray, a few years of dashboard dust and you have the makings of an embarrassing car day.

Professional networkers will often meet and/or carry their conversations into the parking lot. Worse yet, what if your prospect needs a ride? Keeping your car in tip top shape reinforces the good impressions you have been able to establish during your meeting. By the way, if you don't think people are looking at the car you drive, think again. They may not follow you out the door and take notes, but out of the corner of their eye, an impression is formed. Now, we're not saying you have to mortgage the house and buy a brand new Mercedes. However, you should make an effort to keep your car washed, waxed and vacuumed. Many service stations offer a free wash or $1 wash with a fill up. Find one and make it a habit to wash your car every time you fill up.

If you do own a relic and declare your car as a second home on your tax return, then you may want to park in an inconspicuous place. Arrive early and make sure any key contacts you have made at the meeting leave before you do. Remember, nothing you do (including the car you drive) should instill doubt in the prospect's mind. However, if you do have a nice car, with vanity license plates or a van with signage, or even a simple temporary magnetic sign, by all means park it right out front for everyone to see.

Trunk File

One reason why cars get messy fast is that brochures, order forms, cards, and other materials tend to slip and slide when placed on the back seat. One way to ensure that you always have plenty of crisp, organized materials on hand is to develop a trunk file.

Whether you use an old milk crate or a formal flip-top mini file cabinet, stocking one with sales materials and placing it in the trunk of your car will guarantee that you always have the materials you need at hand. Again, after a meeting you may want to run to your car and grab any materials relevant to a conversation you had earlier with certain contacts. This will allow your prospects to return to their offices with your sales materials in hand. While your competition is putting things in the mail, you will be closing the sale.

Things to include in your trunk file are: brochures, business cards, price lists, letterhead, envelopes, stamps, thank you notes, pens, oversized-custom name badge, and yellow pads. Incorporate pink sheets into your file folders. For example, if you keep a stock of 20 order forms in your file, place a pink sheet behind the fifteenth form to remind you to restock when necessary.

In addition to business related items you should also include such ancillary items as: a comb or brush, hair spray, tooth brush, tooth paste, mouthwash, mints, gum, aspirin, cologne, a change of clothes, and a calculator.

Position the trunk file somewhere in your car where it will not tip over or slide as the car turns. The placement of Velcro tape on the bottom of the file will help hook the trunk file to the car's carpeting. If you are using a milk crate, you may also want to design some kind of cover to protect your papers in the event of rain or snow.

Diversify Your Groups

The key to maximizing your exposure and leads that you are able to generate is diversifying your networking groups. A variety of groups exist and you should tap into all of them some of the time and attend others regularly. In the pages that follow, we explain the benefits of membership in each type of group: service groups, Chamber of Commerce/civic groups, lead groups, social groups.

The types of groups you attend will support your networking goals in different ways. The purpose of your networking should be to make it a planned activity versus an arbitrary tool you practice now and then. To get the maximum results from your networking efforts, you should determine the types and number of people you want to meet. If for example accountants are good prospects for you, join or visit groups that comprise accountants. National and local association meetings would be a good place to start. If you are looking for various sized business owners then try a Chamber event.

Finding the groups, it just the first step. Once you get there, you must be specific. In other words, give people the exact title and type of person you are looking for. A vague question like *"Do you know anyone who can help me?"* usually leads to a vague answer like *"Let me think about it."* To make sure this doesn't happen to you, describe your clients in specific terms like Training Directors, Human Resources Directors, Personnel Directors, Meeting Planners, Association Directors, or other high level company personnel.

Whether it is a business or social situation, attend to meet someone new. The more people you know, the more opportunities will come your way.

Service Groups

Service Groups are typically non-profit, volunteer, socially redeeming type organizations. Examples of service type groups include the American Cancer Society, Make a Wish Foundation, Big Brother, Red Cross, Toys for Tots, etc.

Here is how you might benefit from membership in this kind of group. After volunteering for three months at the grass roots level proving your commitment, you may be asked to serve in the capacity of committee chair. As committee chair you may report to the president. Often the president will be a bank president, a company CEO, or a prominent member of the community. Let's assume you sell property and casualty insurance and let's assume you picked a group where the president is the CEO and owner of a large manufacturing facility. As the next six months roll by, you develop a relationship with the CEO on a personal level. Another few months may go by when one day the CEO asks you if you insure large corporate facilities. You, of course act surprised and say "sure, we can handle that" and the CEO invites you to bid on his policy. Your normal volume of policies may be $50 million a year and this one policy may be worth $25 million alone. In retrospect, there is a lot of time and effort invested on your part, but as you can see the payoff can also be worth it. And of course, big fish tend to swim with other big fish. If you do a good job and maintain the relationship, with some effort you will get introduced to some other big fish. Within a matter of a year or two you could double or even triple sales and your income.

Choose the service group you join carefully. Don't only look at presidents, but also at president elects because by the time you make it into the "inner circle" the president who started may be gone. Look for organizations where the prospects are plentiful at many levels and not just concentrated at the very top.

The benefit of joining and volunteering with these groups is the people you will rub elbows with. First and foremost, you must genuinely be prepared to volunteer and contribute the expected amount of time and hours required. Often the more time and effort you are willing to invest, the bigger the decision maker you will get to rub elbows with. Also understand the payoff with these groups is rarely immediate and can take six months to a year to even see the first benefit. Should you decide to take this route, do yourself a favor and research the "big wigs" you will be rubbing elbows with. If they are not your prospects, continue to look for a group until you find one that may benefit your business in some way. Once you have narrowed down a few groups, pick one that you will enjoy as a volunteer. Service group networking is achieved through relationship building and friendships, not outright selling. Don't expect to volunteer for an organization and come home with three hot leads after your first meeting.

Chambers/Civic Groups

Everyone should be an active member of their local Chamber of Commerce. Although some Chambers consist of thousands of members, most consist of hundreds and only a small portion of those are actually active. Consequently, if you are willing to invest the time and effort to attend the monthly meetings, the luncheons and are willing to volunteer for a committee or two, you can get yourself into the inner circle of the Chamber quickly. The secret to maximum Chamber networking is getting to know and developing a genuine relationship with each of the staff members from the receptionist right on up to the president. Remember it is the receptionist who fields the incoming calls from people looking for information. If a caller is looking for a product or service you can provide, it is in your best interest to have your name and number handy.

Join committees that will provide you with the kind of prospects you desire. The Membership Committee is a great way to meet all new businesses coming into the area and the Small Business Committee is a great way to develop relationships with existing business owners.

Regular attendance is key to Chamber recognition. Whenever possible, attend every Chamber event held. Always be on the lookout for new members and guests. Try to be the first person these people meet. Doing so will ease their fear of the unknown and they will appreciate your special attention. They will be loyal to you forever and will look for you at each subsequent meeting. If possible after you have had a chance to indoctrinate them to you and your business, and after you have learned about their business, do your best to introduce them to someone they could do business with. If they walk away from the meeting with a sale in their pocket, or at least a strong lead, they will be loyal to you forever.

Also, go to meetings of the Rotary Club and other civic and fraternal organizations, church groups, trade and professional groups and self-help groups, such as toastmasters. Any type of leadership position in these types of groups will put you in contact with movers and shakers. And, you could have fun doing it.

Lead Groups

A lead group is an organization of people who meet on a regular basis for the sole purpose of exchanging sales leads. Typically, the groups only allow one person from each profession or business category. This ensures that the maximum number of leads get passed with the minimum amount of competition. In addition, each member is encouraged to bring guests and prospective members who may benefit from the group. For example, let's assume you are an accountant and you join a lead group that consists of a real estate agent, an insurance agent, a florist, a chiropractor, a painter, an auto mechanic, and a printer. Each of the members of the group becomes an extended sales arm of the other. So instead of just you out there keeping your ears and eyes open for new business opportunities, you now have seven additional sets of ears and eyes.

Always recommend and promote others in your network. For example, if a client asks you for a product or service you are unable to fulfill, instead of saying you can't handle it, try to match them with other clients and those in your lead group or network. It's great extra value to your existing clients when you can recommend them to someone. Imagine how loyal that client will be.

Here's how it works:

✓ Over the course of the year the real estate agent will help on average three couples who were renting with the purchase of a home. Until their purchase, they did not itemize their tax returns, but with a significant mortgage deduction, closing costs and other moving expenses, they now have a need for an accountant. Knowing this, the real estate agent passes their names and phone number to you as a lead.

✓ The insurance agent one day fields inquiries from a client who wants insurance quotes should they decide to rent their house to a tenant. The client also inquires about whether or not rates will increase or decrease on homes in a neighboring community. The insurance agent puts two and two together and confirms his clients are thinking about moving, that they currently do not have an agent and would be interested in being contacted by an agent who specializes in single family home sales.

✓ The chiropractor, while working on an elderly patient with lower back pain, learns the patient wants to sell her three story townhouse and move into a condo. The patient complains that the constant stair climbing aggravates her back condition and that now would be a good time to sell. The chiropractor confirms that the patient is currently working with another agent and asks if she would like to be contacted by a friend of hers. The patient appreciates the referral.

✓ The scenario goes on and on. In the Fall, the painter paints the home of a family looking to sell in the Spring. The florist sends flowers to a widower whose spouse recently died and will be moving in with family members across town. The mechanic works on the car of a person who complains that his long distance commute creates too much wear and tear on his car. And, the printer learns that one of his customers making photocopies of an upcoming garage sale is planning to put his house on the market after he sells off 20 years worth of accumulated stuff.

Over the course of a year, you will probably attain at least one solid sales lead from each person in the group. Depending on the person and how complimentary the profession is to yours, you may receive upwards of five or more from a single member. As you know, a hot prospect referral is the equivalent to making 100 phone calls or mailing out 1,000 mail pieces. Membership in a lead group like this could double or even triple your sales over the course of a year.

Remember the sales leads must flow the other way too. Every customer you sell a home too, with the buyer's permission, would become a lead for the insurance agent in the group. During a listing appointment, you suggest the prospective seller paint the kitchen and master bedroom and suggest a painter who will give them a good price, etc.

In the above scenario, the lead group was made up of seven people. We belong to groups made up of more than 30. In addition, you may want to join multiple lead groups located in different areas of town with different members.

Lead groups work best when the members meet weekly, enforce mandatory attendance, chart and make public among group members the number of (good) leads each person in the group passes. The only cost associated with some groups is the cost of your breakfast or lunch each week. Other groups charge a small annual fee to cover minor expenses such as advertising, trade show booths and parties. And yet, others are "for-profit" and charge accordingly.

If you are unaware of lead groups existing in your area, check with your local Chamber of Commerce as well as local diners, restaurants and hotels. Most meet for breakfast at 7 AM or so on a weekly basis, others meet for lunch and still others meet after the business day. If you can't find a group, gather 8 or 10 compatible business people and start your own group.

	TTL YTD	TTL WKL	ON TIME 1 2 3 4 5	ATTEND 1 2 3 4 5 6	GUESTS 1 2 3 4 5	LEADS 1 2 3 4 5	MEMBERS 1 2 3 4 5 6
ARVANITIS, VIC	7	0	N N N N N	1 1 0 1 1	0 0 0 0 0	0 3 0 0 0	0 0 0 0 0
BROWN, JOHN	2	2	N N N N N	1 1 0 0 0	0 0 0 0 0	0 0 0 0 0	0 0 0 0 0
EAGER, JEANNE	7	5	N N N N N	1 1 1 1 0	0 0 0 0 0	0 3 0 0 0	0 0 0 0 0
CLARK, LYNNE	19	2	N N N Y N	1 1 1 1 0	0 0 0 0 0	9 0 3 3 0	0 0 0 0 0
COFFEY, RANDY	8	5	N Y N N N	1 1 0 0 0	0 0 0 0 0	3 3 0 0 0	0 0 0 0 0
DONAHUE, JUDY	19	5	N N N Y Y	1 1 0 1 1	0 0 0 0 0	0 3 9 0 3	0 0 0 0 0
FAIRCHILD, CECILIA	18	2	N N N N Y	1 1 0 1 1	0 0 5 0 0	0 0 0 9 0	0 0 0 0 0
FENTON, PATRICIA	14	2	N N N N Y	1 1 1 1 1	0 0 0 0 0	3 0 3 3 0	0 0 0 0 0
FRESH, ERIN	10	4	N Y Y Y Y	0 1 1 1 1	0 0 0 0 0	0 3 0 3 0	0 0 0 0 0
GILL, DENNIS	4	2	N N Y N Y	1 1 1 0 1	0 0 0 0 0	0 0 0 0 0	0 0 0 0 0
GILLEN, KATHY	20	7	Y Y N N Y	1 1 0 1 1	5 0 0 0 0	3 0 0 0 3	0 5 0 0 0
GILLEN, MARY	18	2	Y N N N N	1 1 1 1 0	0 0 5 0 0	0 0 9 0 0	0 0 0 0 0
GOULDIN, JOHN	14	2	Y Y Y Y Y	1 1 1 1 1	0 0 0 0 0	6 0 0 3 0	0 0 0 0 0
HENRY, ROY	8	0	N Y N N N	0 0 0 1 1	0 0 0 0 0	0 0 0 6 0	0 0 0 0 0
HOWARD, BILL	18	5	N N N N Y	1 1 1 0 1	0 0 0 0 5	0 3 3 0 3	0 0 0 0 0
HOWELL, RALPH	8	2	N N N Y Y	1 1 1 1 1	0 0 0 0 0	3 0 0 0 0	0 0 0 0 0
ILVENTO, JOE	32	5	Y N Y N Y	1 1 1 1 1	0 0 0 0 0	6 3 3 6 9	0 0 0 0 0
JOHNSON, CAROL	38	8	Y Y Y Y Y	1 1 1 1 1	0 0 0 0 0	6 6 6 6 9	0 0 0 0 0
KRAWCYZK, LORRAINE	9	2	N N N Y Y	1 1 1 0 1	0 0 0 0 5	0 0 0 0 0	0 0 0 0 0
KAISER, NED	7	2	N N Y N Y	1 1 1 0 1	0 0 0 0 0	0 0 3 0 0	0 0 0 0 0
LOVE, JOE	23	14	N N N Y Y	1 1 1 1 1	0 0 0 0 0	3 12 3 0 0	0 0 0 0 0
McGRANIHAN, BUD	4	1	N Y Y Y Y	0 1 1 1 1	0 0 0 0 0	0 0 0 0 0	0 0 0 0 0
MASON, DICK	13	2	Y Y Y N Y	1 1 1 0 1	0 0 0 0 0	3 0 6 0 0	0 0 0 0 0
RAGSDALE, BARBARA	14	8	N Y Y Y Y	1 1 1 1 1	0 0 0 0 0	0 6 0 3 0	0 0 0 0 0
RENOLDS, NICK	5	2	N N Y Y Y	1 1 1 1 1	0 0 0 0 0	0 0 0 0 0	0 0 0 0 0
SPAC, LAURA	47	8	N N N Y Y	1 1 1 1 1	0 0 0 0 0	6 6 3 9 18	0 0 0 0 0
SNOW, CARL	37	11	Y Y Y Y Y	1 1 1 1 1	0 0 5 0 0	0 9 0 3 15	0 0 0 0 0
SOARD, CHARLIE	6	2	Y N N Y N	1 1 0 1 0	0 0 0 0 0	0 0 0 3 0	0 0 0 0 0
SOARD, JO	19	2	Y N Y Y N	1 1 1 1 0	0 0 0 0 0	12 0 3 0 0	0 0 0 0 0
COTTON, BRETT	10	5	Y Y N Y Y	1 1 0 1 1	0 0 0 0 0	0 3 0 0 0	0 0 0 0 0
VESEY, BILL	6	2	Y Y N N Y	1 1 0 0 1	0 0 0 0 0	0 0 0 0 3	0 0 0 0 0
VORACEK, DAVE	16	2	Y N Y Y N	1 1 1 1 0	0 0 0 0 0	12 0 0 0 0	0 0 0 0 0
WAITSCHIES, GARY	12	4	N Y Y Y Y	0 1 1 1 1	0 0 0 0 5	0 3 0 0 0	0 0 0 0 0
WINSOR, PETER	9	0	N N Y Y N	0 0 1 1 1	0 0 0 0 0	0 0 3 3 0	0 0 0 0 0
WEBER, CHARNEY	14	2	Y Y Y Y Y	1 1 1 1 1	0 0 0 0 0	6 0 3 0 0	0 0 0 0 0
WEST, PAT	3	1	N N N N N	1 0 0 1 1	0 0 0 0 0	0 0 0 0 0	0 0 0 0 0

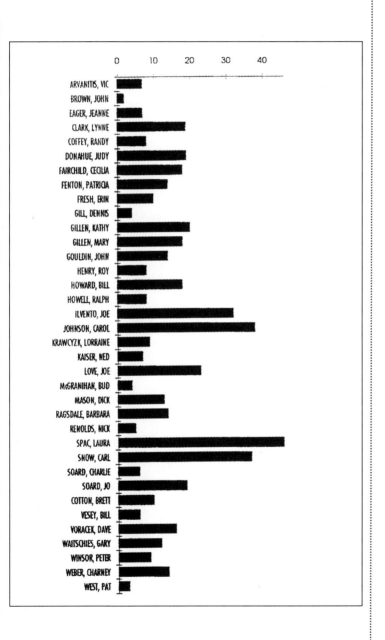

Social Events

Social events like weddings, cocktail receptions, corporate parties, or any type of gathering are potential networking events. Take advantage of these opportunities to find out the businesses of those seated at your table or attending the same party. Remember, someone's friend or relative may be your next prospect or better yet a source of hundreds of referrals.

The bottom line in these types of situations is to make friends. Don't push yourself on others. Find out what you have in common with someone and how you could help each other.

Whether it is a business or social situation and you want to meet someone, just do it. The more people you know the more opportunities will come your way.

Name Badge

One of the best, easiest and inexpensive ways to get yourself noticed at a networking event is the use of a name badge. It is real easy to spot the professional networkers in a crowd. They typically are the ones with the custom name badges. Whenever possible, stay away from the "Hello my Name Is..." fill in the blank type tags common at many events. If you must use one, or for whatever reason you don't want to call attention to yourself and blend into the crowd, print your name and company name neatly on the badge. If you have horrible handwriting and you are not a doctor, get one of the event organizers to print your name on the badge for you. Remember, first impressions count and the last thing you want to be labeled is sloppy or incompetent.

The best name badges we have seen are the ones you make yourself. Little did I know how successful my badge was going to be until the next meeting I attended after wearing it the first time. Not thinking it was important, I did not wear the badge a second time. It was only after three different people came up to me and asked me where my badge was did I realize how much power it had at getting me noticed. The fact is I needed a badge for an upcoming trade show. I wanted it to match a guerrilla marketing theme I was using at the show so I combined a 3 x 3 inch photo of a guerrilla with my name, company name and a "Ask Me How..." type question. A few things happened the minute I put it on. First, as people approached me they all took the time to first comment on the picture and then came even closer to read the message. Second, because the picture of a guerrilla was unique and funny, it brought a smile to their faces. Third, the badge became the initial topic of conversation and then we moved to the business at hand. And finally, the badge earned me an instant reputation and I have since worn it to every major networking event I have attended with similar results.

To reduce the wear and tear on your clothes, use a magnetic name badge. Pick the two oldest magnets off your refrigerator and glue one magnet to the back of your badge and place the other magnet under your blouse or lapel.

Make your name badge an advertising piece. An art gallery owner made her badge into a little gilded art frame. Instead of Mona Lisa you see her picture and name. Or, wear an interesting button. We've seen people wearing buttons that say, "Ask me how to make $,1000" or just "Ask Me..." It's a great way to start a conversation.

Or, if you have a badge in which you write in your name and title, do more! Instead of just putting your title or business, put something like "Problem Solver" or "Money Maker." These quotes get people curious to find out what you do.

If possible, stay away from the small business card size badges. This format is too small and most people do the obvious and slip their business card into the plastic holder. Have you ever tried to read the print on a business card from 5 feet away? If you aren't familiar with some of the desk top publishing software programs on the market today, find someone who is. Have them create a custom name tag for you complete with a relevant photo and output it on a color printer. Pick up a large 3 x 4 inch or 4 x 5 inch plastic name tag holder and insert the custom piece inside the holder. You may want to make few and place one in the breast pocket of all your suits, put one in your trunk file and keep one in your brief case.

Hand-Outs

The professional networker does not want to be slowed down by bulky hand-outs. The last thing you want to do is to show up at a cocktail reception with large brochures touting the benefits of your products and services. First, bulky brochures and flyers require at least one hand to hold. Assuming you have a drink or a cup of coffee in the other, you are left handless to meet and shake hands with new people. Not to mention people looking at you will label you as unapproachable. Why? First, because you have no free hands. Second, is the fact that you are broadcasting that if you meet me I'm going to give you one of these bulky brochures. Now, they get stuck carrying it around. Often, the brochure will be put down at the earliest convenience and odds are it will never be seen again.

If you have to bring materials with you, put them down somewhere in the room in a conspicuous place. As you meet and greet people, let them know where they can pick up one of your brochures if they are genuinely interested. Better yet, mail them one or offer to personally drop it off so your sales message is not mixed with all the new names and information the person has processed at the event.

If possible, create brochures in a tri-fold type format which fits into the breast pocket of a men's suit. This allows you to carry materials on you and keep both hands free, plus, it's easy for the prospect to carry.

For weekly events, like a lead group, a hand-out is an inexpensive way to get those in attendance to walk away with something with your name on it. These are what are called "throw aways" so depending on your budget, don't be offended if you find some get left behind, some end up in the trash and some get forever filed away.

To reduce the "throw away" factor you must do your best to make the information useful. If you meet on a weekly basis create a hand-out that provides your business information on one side and provides a valuable marketing or sales tip on the other. We suggest that you print three or four tips to a standard 8 1/2 x 11 inch page. Use color paper and run it through your laser printer. If you like, number the tips 1-52 and hand out a new one each week. Rather than be viewed as trash, now your hand-out will be viewed as cash!

Business Cards

A business card is the professional networkers most effective and least expensive tool. Make your business card stand out from all the others. If you were to lay down 20 business cards of the people you met at the last networking event you attended, based on the look of the business card alone, who would you do business with? What does the card say to you? Was it professionally produced? What was the paper weight used? Did it have a gloss to it? Was it multi-colored? Did it contain a photo? Was there useful information on the back of the card? Did it fold? Was it a non-standard size? Did it contain metallic ink? Was the typeface unique? Did it contain the person's e-mail address or web page?

When you think about it, there is probably not one single piece of material that is distributed more to your prospects than your business card. Yet most people invest little time and expense in developing an effective card.

A good business card is one that is both functional and yet memorable. Choose a paper that parallels the image you want your customers to feel when holding it. Flannel papers give a soft, easy feeling. Coated papers give a sharp, crisp feeling. And the use of recycled paper shows that you care about the environment. Carefully pick your ink colors too. Do you have corporate colors? Metallic and bright colored inks get the reader's attention. Muted soft colored inks send a more subtle message. And finally, make your card functional. Does it include all the information a person needs to reach you? The inclusion of e-mail addresses is becoming more popular these days. If you have one use it. Is there a coupon, map, price list, or some other valuable information on the back of the card that gives the reader an additional reason to save it? If you like, you can make your business card a mini step brochure offering the reader features, benefits, price lists, coupons, tips, etc. For example, the back of an attorney's business card could list tips on what to do if you are arrested. The back of an insurance agent's card could offer tips on what to do if in an accident.

If you haven't done so already, take a moment to critique your business card and make any and all improvements you see fit. Remember, on a cost per unit basis, your business card is the most effective marketing and networking tool you have available.

Dress Professionally

Another key trait of a professional networker is the manner in which they dress. In a networking environment, you work and sell in a matter of minutes, not hours, so the impression you leave with your prospect is very important. Studies show that close to 50% of a person's first impression of you is based on visual cues. Therefore, the way you look and dress can dramatically enhance your status and credibility in the prospect's mind. This doesn't mean you have to buy $800 Italian suits. However, what you do wear should not detract from your overall message.

Some of the dress professional basics include: polished shoes, a neatly pressed suit, a 100% cotton shirt, no wrinkles, a nice tie, a matching belt, a good haircut, neatly trimmed fingernails, a decent watch. The same holds true for women with a few exceptions, specifically replacing the 100% cotton shirt with a nice blouse, and the tie with an optional scarf.

The professional networker looks at his or her appearance as a total package and understands that one flaw can spoil the entire first impression. The concept of congruence comes into play when meeting people for the first time. People, based on their past experiences and preconceived notions, whether right or wrong, have an image in their mind of what a successful attorney, accountant, or building contractor looks like. One dress component out of place can create doubt and consequently a hesitation to do business with you. For example, scuffed or unpolished shoes, a cheap watch with a broken wrist band, or dirty fingernails may cause you to doubt the validity and genuineness of all the other dress components. Rather than walking away impressed with a willingness to do business with this person, you are hesitant and will want to learn more about him or her before proceeding any further with the relationship.

Is this to say that just because a person has unpolished shoes one day that you never do business with them? Of course not, however, a professional networker understands that in the majority of cases many of the contacts they make will be one time face-to-face meetings and the relationship that follows will be developed over the phone and by mail. Failure to maximize that initial and critical face-to-face encounter may forever taint the phone and mail relationship. Recovering from a poor first impression may take months or even years to overcome. Therefore, it is in your best interest to ensure that your first impression is a perfect one.

Create an Identity

One of the most powerful things you can do as a professional networker to distinguish yourself within a crowd of people is to create an identity for yourself. One gentleman we know helps people redesign their ailing brochures. Appropriately, he calls himself the "Brochure Doctor" and wears a white doctors coat and stethoscope around his neck. If you see him again across the room at another networking function, do you think you will remember what he does for a living? In other words, if possible, don't just become another stuffed suit.

One reason many people have trouble remembering names in networking environments is because everyone tends to look the same. Be different! Have fun! If you are an aggressive trial attorney and present yourself as such, wear a shark hat. If you sell chocolates, why not give people a chocolate business card with a real one attached to it. If your product or service saves people money, wear a tie or scarf imprinted with hundred dollar bills. Dare to be different and you will instantly have everyone's attention. Hats, ties, scarfs, lapel pins, tie clips, business cards, hand-outs, and name badges are just a few of the ways you can be sure to get yourself noticed and more importantly, known.

Once you have a theme or gimmick, thread it through your promotional materials. Capture the theme in graphic form or in a catchy slogan and use it on your business cards, letterhead, envelopes, and promotional materials. People remember pictures and images more than names. Soon you will develop a reputation. People who have attended the event will talk about you, and those you've never met will say that they have heard of you from friends and associates. Never again will you be at a loss for words when you meet people for the first time.

NetWORKING

We are amazed at the number of people who attend critical networking events and spend the majority of their time looking for a cup of coffee, a drink or something to eat. The professional networker understands what networking is all about — working and not eating and drinking. To appease your hunger pains and desire for caffeine, eat and drink prior to the event.

The benefits of this technique will more than pay for itself time and time again. First, it allows you to keep your hands free at all times to meet, greet and obtain cards from the maximum number of people in the room. Having a second hand free will allow you to take notes directly on the person's business card and also make any special notes on your card before giving it to the prospect.

Because many networking events are only an hour or so in length, upwards of 15% to 25% of your time can be spent ordering, drinking and eating at the event. Investing this valuable time into meeting new contacts will increase your contact base by an equal or greater percentage.

▲

Networking Protocol

The best way to get yourself blackballed from a net-working event is to overstep your boundaries during the opportunity you are given to introduce yourself. Many events will provide a time when guests are given a minute or so to briefly introduce themselves to the group. For most, they do not use this minute to its max-imum potential. However, some abuse the opportunity and literally talk themselves right out of the possibility of making even one contact. Their one minute introduction quickly evolves into a 10 minute presentation. Professional networking can be measured in minutes. Since most meetings are only 90 minutes in length, going over your allotted time by 9 minutes means you wasted 10% of the meeting's networking potential.

Before attending an event or prior to being introduced to the group, confirm the protocol of guest introductions such as:

✓ How long do you have to speak?

✓ What typically do people say?

✓ Are their any forbidden topics?

Usually, you will want to confidently introduce your-self, the name of your company, a general benefit of how you have been able to help other business owners, and finish off with the kind of prospects you are looking for. Don't talk too long, *stay focused on your primary busi-ness* and try not to overlap into product lines and ser-vices already provided by members of the group. One key to being successful in a networking group is by earn-ing the credibility and trust of the others. If you say you do one thing, and then introduce a side business, it may appear to others that you are not successful in your primary business and consequently need a second or third income to pay the bills. With regards to networking, a primary business is not necessarily the business that provides you with your greatest source of income, but the business category you filled or joined under when becoming a member of the networking group. Typically the more exclusive the group, such as a lead group, the more likely they will only allow you to speak about your primary business.

Side businesses range from gourmet cake baking to network marketing opportunities. There is nothing wrong with having a side business. As a matter of fact, for some, these side businesses are their primary source of income. However, if you want to talk about your side business there are a couple of tips to keep in mind.

First, check the group's policies on talking about anything other than the primary business category you filled when joining the group. If there is a policy that prevents you from telling others about your side business during the meeting, it is best to meet or contact the members on a one-on-one basis before or after the meeting.

Second, if you want to officially speak about your side business, either re-join your existing group under the category of your side business, visit as a guest, or join as a member of other networking groups under your side business category. This approach will provide you with the credibility and trust that comes with the introduction of a single primary business.

▲

Practice Your Presentation

The time to perfect your presentation is prior to the networking event. As you will see in a later chapter, a good networking presentation is one that is concise and to-the-point. People like brevity and the shorter your presentation, the more impact it will have on the prospect. For the most part, you are introducing yourself, your company, a general benefit of your product or service and finishing up with the kind of prospects you are looking for. This process takes approximately one minute to complete.

Tailor your general benefit statement to either the prospect or group you are addressing. For example, if you are a copier salesperson addressing a group of small business owners you might say something like, *"Good Morning, my name is Joe Smith and I represent ZYX Copier company. ZYX is unique in the copier business because we specialize in serving the needs of small business owners like yourself. We offer a free toner package and up to 5,000 sheets of premium copier paper for businesses with annual sales less than $2 million. If you know of a small business owner who would like to take advantage of this great small business offer, please call me at the number found on my business card."*

If meeting one-on-one with an insurance agent you might say, *"Good Morning, my name is Joe Smith and I represent ZYX Copier company. ZYX is unique in the copier business because we specialize in serving the needs of insurance agents like yourself. We offer a free toner package and up to 5,000 sheets of premium copier paper for businesses with annual revenues of less than $2 million. Here is my card, if you or another agent you know would like to take advantage of this one time special offer, please contact me at your convenience."*

The basic presentation follows a simple formula that is altered depending on the person or group you are addressing:

✓ Practice the presentation until you feel comfortable saying it and can say it like you mean it.

✓ Practice inflection, pauses and tempo.

✓ Practice altering the offer and the benefit statement.

✓ Practice customizing it to a variety of common business people you come in contact with on a regular basis. How would you customize for an accountant, an attorney, a new car dealer, a florist, a printer, a convenience store owner, a hair dresser, etc.

With practice, you'll be able to customize a powerful presentation on the fly and never again will you feel awkward or nervous when it comes your time to introduce yourself to a crowd of 1 or 100.

Vary Your 1 Minute Presentation

There is nothing worse than to attend a networking function with the same 20 people for five years only to hear the same presentation over and over again. Do yourself and your fellow networkers a favor and mix it up a little.

The easiest way to vary your presentation is to tell a story about your latest customers. Review with the group the customer's unique needs and how you helped them. Using this approach will ensure every presentation you make is a unique and interesting one.

A stock broker might give a tip of the week and tell the group what they would have made (or lost) if they invested $1,000. A florist might bring a new kind of flower to talk about. An insurance agent could bring pictures of property damage and car accidents.

Inviting Guests

The expert networker knows his or her success at any networking event is based on the total number of new and existing contacts he or she is able to make. The more people at the event, who know and talk about you, the more leads for your products and services will be generated. One technique to tip the attendance profile of a networking event in your favor is to invite as many guests to the event as possible. Business people are always looking for opportunities to meet others so your invitation to attend a local networking event will be viewed as a positive.

With the popularity of fax software and fax modems in today's computers, inviting 50 or so guests to an event can be as simple as the flip of a switch.

For those of you who do not have access to this technology, the creation and mailing of a postcard with the event information is the next best thing. Gather the names, numbers and address information of people you know and have recently met at other networking events and incorporate this information into a fax or mailing label database. This will allow you to create one invitation and fax or mail it to everyone on your list. This technique is ideal for larger chamber and social events where you will be either attending or featured as a guest speaker.

Imagine you're in a room of 50 people and 15 of those individuals were invited by you. We have always found that the people you invite appreciate the opportunity to meet new people and those you did not invite appreciate the opportunity to meet your guests. Sooner or later how they learned about the event will come up in conversation and your name will be mentioned time and time again.

Turning Salespeople into Gold

When was the last time you were happy to receive a phone call from a salesperson trying to sell you something? We have found salespeople to be an endless supply of guests we can bring to networking events and lead groups. Often their goal is to meet with you face to face and try to sell you their product or service. If you know of an upcoming event, invite the salesperson to the event as your guest. If you are not interested in their product or service, invite them anyway, with the allure that there may be 20 or so other people at the meeting who may be interested in what they have to sell.

Chambers and lead groups encourage this kind of invitation and in many cases you may receive some kind of credit in the event your guest decides to become a member of the group. Again, the salesperson will appreciate the opportunity to meet 20 new prospects and usually a few existing members of the group genuinely have a need for the product or service being offered.

Often, we will trade the salesperson's invitation for a solid lead or a "quid pro quo" type of deal. For example, if I introduce you to 20 new prospects, will you do your best to send me three or four prospects in the next couple of weeks? Don't be surprised if the salesperson gives you a couple of names of people to call over the phone.

Never again will you want those annoying telemarketing and cold call canvassers to stop calling on you. Remember these kinds of salespeople are often the best kind to know. Because it is their job to contact hundreds of new prospects each week, you can benefit greatly from their contact base. Often the objections to their product or services can be transformed into leads for you. For example, a copier salesperson who hears *"We are not interested in a new mega-copier because we plan to out-source all our mega-copies to a copy center"* now has a golden lead to trade to a copy center owner for a lead of a former customer who is considering bringing their copying requirements in-house.

Profile of Customers

It is essential to know yourself and your customers to make your networking generate the effects you want. A marketing audit will help you recognize an opportunity when you see it. In addition, you will be able to target the who, what, where, why, and when of successful networking. To avoid arbitrary decisions, get solid marketing information and move your business and career to new levels.

Your answers to the following key questions will provide the basis for your marketing audit:

✓ *What business am I really in?* By realizing the clients needs that your business meets your marketing strategy will focus on your true competition.

✓ *Where can I diversify?* You need to consider additional services you can offer to your customers.

✓ *What is the perceived quality of the service or merchandise I sell?* People buy for their reasons, not ours. The customer is the one who really defines quality.

✓ *What kind of image do I want to project?* One of the keys to offering a successful product or service is to position it in the mind of the customer. The marketing term positioning means how you want your product or service to be seen in the eyes of the consumer.

✓ *How do I compare with the competition?* There are three reasons why you need to know about your competition. The first is to determine where you have the advantages. The second is to know why and how they are better. The third is to copy success. In other words, produce the same results that successful people produce and you too will be successful. Some of the areas where you need to compare yourself with the competition are product, price, promotion, place, package, and personnel.

✓ *What benefits do I offer my customers?* What can your clients save, gain, accomplish, or avoid by using your product or service?

✓ *Who are my customers?* You need to focus on the 20% of your customers that give you 80% of your income. Characteristics to focus on include age, income, geographic region, lifestyle, attitudes, usage patterns.

✓ *Can they afford our product or service?* Do you have different services and products to meet the needs of various market segments?

✓ *When do they buy your product or service?* You'll know the best times to market your product or service by understanding key buying times for your clients and customers.

✓ *Why do they buy from me?* What makes you unique or different? This is your Unique Selling Position (USP). Uniqueness could be as simple as being able to consult with clients late at night or perhaps a dentist who offers the use of his fax machine and telephone while a patient is waiting for an appointment.

Network with Competitors

By developing a trusting relationship with your competitors, it's amazing how you want help each other. For example, we sometimes decline certain jobs because we don't have the time or inclination. By referring it to our competitor, everybody wins. The client gets the service he or she wants. The competitor gets the work. And we get goodwill and a referral fee from our competitor. Also, the competitor's we work with understand that this is *our* client and any request for future work must come through us first.

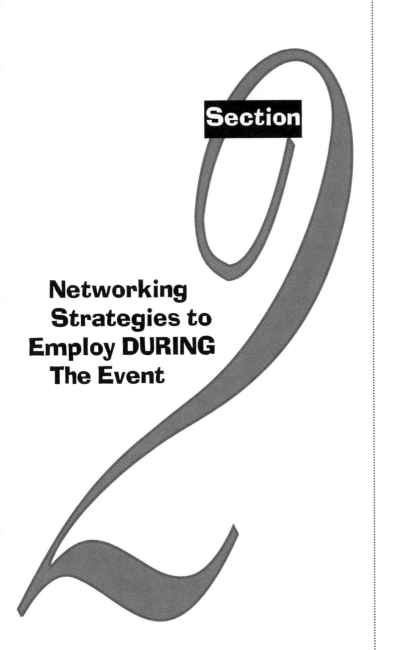

Section

Networking Strategies to Employ DURING The Event

Act Like You Own the Place

When attending a networking event you need to possess the right attitude. It is not easy to walk into a room full of complete strangers and strike up meaningful business conversations. So what better attitude to take than to act as if you own the place. Rather than look like a scared guest, act as if you were the host. Think of the gathering as your event and it is your job to meet, greet and make everybody feel at home. Just introduce yourself to the first stranger you see. After the first or second introduction, the rest are easy.

A Good Lead for Me Is . . .

It's up to you to let others know the kind of business you desire. The best way to do this is to just come right out and say it. Simply make the first or last words of your presentation, *"A good lead for me is....,"* and of course add the kinds of customers you desire.

Meet Everyone, An UP is an UP is an UP

Do you have any preconceived notions? Do you judge people by the way they look, dress and talk? If you are like most people, you probably do. Unfortunately, doing so will lead to your competition scooping up sales right from under your nose. Early in my sales career, I was fortunate to work in a selling environment where we didn't choose the prospects, but worked on a wheel system in which the best salesperson was assigned the first customer, the next best salesperson was assigned the second customer and so on.

However, we quickly learned that whether or not a person bought had nothing to do with the way they looked, talked or dressed. Everyone who walked through that door was considered to be an Unqualified Prospect or an *UP*. After we had a chance to determine their exact needs did they turn into qualified prospects and eventually customers. However, an *UP* was an *UP* was an *UP*. Just as many people without suits and ties bought the product as those with suits and ties.

Don't allow yourself to prejudge a prospect at a networking event. Just think an *UP* is an *UP* is an *UP*. Because so many other people are afraid to speak to someone who doesn't appear to be qualified, that person is usually one of the easiest to sell because they are unaware of your competition.

During a networking event, your goal is to meet everyone you have not met before, regardless of what they look like. Doing so will ensure the maximum number of new contacts are made and will prove to you time and time again that "diamonds in the rough" really do exist.

Become a Desired Commodity

Are you viewed as a resource by those who know you? Do people call you frequently for your advice and opinions? If not, you need to add more value to everything and everyone you come in contact with. Do not hesitate to share your expert insights with others regarding a subject in your field of work. Don't worry about revealing trade secrets or not being compensated for giving free advice. A good networker is known as someone who is approachable and one who freely and willingly answers the questions of others.

Gaining the reputation of "answer man" will have people approaching you with their questions at events and long after the meetings are over. However, the person who calls about a little question often has a big question lying underneath. Little questions are usually not billable, but the big questions are almost always billable. Whether you are an auto mechanic or an attorney, if people know they can call you and get their questions answered, then soon you will be on the road to a steady flow of queries for your service. You will become a desired commodity.

You will find that many people will call you just to get the names and numbers of others. That's OK. Why? Because they are getting into the habit of when they need good information or recommendations, they call you. You in turn can parlay that lead into three or four referrals to those in your network. (see *Leveraging Your Leads*)

The key to using this technique is to not expect any immediate returns. Over time, people will begin to value your expertise. Once you become the expert, the phone calls are sure to follow.

Ask for Referrals

It is a common pitfall for many salespeople to forget to ask for the order. They talk and talk and present benefit after benefit, but never come right out and ask for the order. Well, the same holds true with referrals. Salespeople who have finally learned to ask for the order forget to ask for referrals.

Referrals are the easiest way to double and even triple sales in the shortest period of time available to you today. Imagine if you only sell one out of every three referrals you get, that's like making each 1 sale the equivalent of 1.33 sales. That's one free sale for every three you make. And remember, that's with no mass calling, no mass telemarketing and no mass mailings.

Referrals are easy to obtain once you know how. One of the easiest people to get referrals from are people who do not need your product or service at this point in time. Naturally they want to help, so in response to your question of who else they might know who could use the product or service, often 3 or 4 names will come fourth. Another technique, is to appeal to the prospect's stomach. Create a post card that features your name and address pre-printed on one side and on the other side in big bold letters at the top reads "THIS CARD IS WORTH DINNER FOR TWO." Follow that with a list of local restaurants the prospect can choose from and note that to obtain the free dinner certificate the postcard must be filled out in full and no lines can be left blank. You then follow that with 10 sets of boxes that each includes space for the prospect to write the contact's first name, contact's last name, title, company name, brief description of business, mailing address, phone and fax.

Another effective technique is "vertical referrals." This approach has you focus on a particular vertical market such as doctors, car dealers, accountants, insurance agents, etc. You simply ask everyone you know to provide you with the name of their doctor, accountant, insurance agent, etc. You then develop a custom mail piece or telephone script geared toward the vertical market.

▲

Ask Provocative Questions

One way to get yourself noticed and even into the local newspaper is to ask provocative questions. The kind of question you ask tells others a lot about you. And asking the right question at the right time can establish credibility with the audience. With regards to the newspaper, you can bet that if the Chamber of Commerce invites a Congressman or the Governor to speak to the group, the news media will be there. Because one of the ultimate goals of networking is to make yourself known to others, a photo in the newspaper or a clip of you asking a question on the local TV news is a great way to do it.

The amount of effort and thought (and nerve) that goes into preparing a question, typically is in direct proportion to the speaker's notoriety. More thought should go into asking the Governor the right question than into a question directed at a local Councilman. In other words, you want to do your homework. Because the purpose of the question is designed to be provocative and be repeated in the news media, ask a relevant question on behalf of the community. Unfortunately, the more controversial the question, the more likely it will make the news. A safe question might address what the speaker's thoughts are regarding the local business community.

If you are the networking event organizer and you plan to have a prominent speaker orate at the meeting, don't forget to invite the press. Seek someone with a public relations background and have them prepare a press release or press kit. Doing so will ensure they understand the purpose of the meeting, the speech highlights and most importantly, they will know how to spell your name right.

Whether you are in a group of 10 or 1,000, formulating and asking a provocative question is an easy way to get yourself noticed. Newsworthy events that allow you to fire off a provocative question are far and few between, so be sure you capitalize on the event.

Become an Officer or Get to Know One

Almost every organization you may belong to has some form of elected or appointed leadership. officer, president, vice president, ambassador, and chairman are just a few of the more familiar high profile positions you might strive to attain. Although the process of becoming an officer of the organization is typically done prior to the meeting, the benefits of being an officer are highlighted during the meeting.

As the president, often it is you who leads the events, runs the meetings, presents the awards, appears on the local TV news, gets quoted in the local and regional newspapers, and appoints many of the sub-positions below you. However, don't kid yourself, becoming the president of an organization is hard work and requires a significant investment of your free time and effort. Make sure you genuinely understand what is expected of any position before getting appointed.

There may be other positions that are not as time consuming and yet will yield comparable results. Many Chambers and organizations will have a Membership Committee. As the chairman or member of the Membership Committee, your task will be to contact and recruit prospective members. This is a great position to be in if you want to reach the maximum number of new business contacts in the community. You will be given access to the organization's existing membership directory as well as additional databases and lists of new and existing business owners. The benefit is that you not only have the name, addresses and telephone numbers of existing members, but also the even bigger list of businesses that for whatever reason, decide not to join.

Another good position to volunteer for is that of ambassador. The title may vary by organization, but for the most part, ambassadors are tasked with the set-up, logistics and break down of each event the organization sponsors. Often, ambassadors' fees to attend the meetings, luncheons, dinners, golf tournaments, etc., are waived because they are considered to be "working" for the event. Ambassadors are the people who meet and make guests feel welcome at events, they keep track of the president and make sure the meeting runs according to schedule.

In the event you are attending a function for the first time and you want to maximize the time available to make new contacts, find an ambassador or officer, introduce yourself, tell them the kind of people you are looking to meet and they will gladly make some introductions for you. This technique can save you countless hours and ensure you do not let key prospects slip through the door because you did not get an opportunity to meet everyone in the room.

Body Language

Body language, as in any social situation, is especially important during networking events. Because you have only a limited time to make an impression on the prospects you are meeting for the first time, your body language must be congruent with the positive way you look and speak.

Because many people are always on the lookout for who else is walking into the room, they fail to maintain eye contact with the person they are speaking with. Not that you want to stare, but 90 percent of the time your eyes should be on the prospect. If you are easily distracted position yourself so that your back is to the rest of the room. On the other hand, it is usually best to position yourself so you face the room. Occasionally, you can glance up to notice any newcomers entering the room, but more importantly you want others to see you.

Most people are right handed and therefore are right eye dominant. Pick an eye and stick with it for the entire conversation. When talking to people up close, rapid eye movements from eye-to-eye and eye-to-mouth can be distracting to the other person.

When speaking to someone for the first time, lean slightly forward to show interest. Clarify and confirm as needed to illustrate that you genuinely understand the points the other person is making. Never keep both hands in both pockets; one hand in a pocket, on occasion, is OK. Remove all keys, loose change, bulky wallets, etc., from your pockets so you are not bulging at the seams. Take some cash, business cards, a credit card and your car key with you and leave everything else in your car.

Positive body language is a sign that a person is interested in what you are saying. To ensure that someone is interested, look for the following signs. Are they:

✓ Asking specific questions?

✓ Maintaining eye contact with you?

✓ Using hand gestures to illustrate a point?

✓ Listening to what you are saying?

✓ Taking notes?

✓ Suggesting future times and dates when you can get together?

Be careful not to place too much emphasis on body language. Bad news at home, a headache or cold can temporarily affect the way people interpersonally communicate. Don't assume disinterest too fast without carefully considering all possibilities.

Card Games

To make each and every networking event you attend fun and exciting, you may want to play a few business card games. One game we play is to see how many new people we can meet and new business cards we can obtain in the shortest period of time. Spend only a minute or so with each new person, get their card and then move on to the next person.

We can't tell you how many people we know attend networking events and leave with only one or two cards out of a room of 50 or more people. Professional networkers know that the sale and relationship begin after the initial contact is made and that the person's business card is your only link to that person once you have left the event.

Another technique you can use to obtain business cards is to give away a door prize at the event. The door prize should appeal to the maximum number of attendees to ensure the greatest participation. If you are a financial planner, don't give away a free personal financial plan. Savvy business people can see right through that scheme and know it's only going to be a thinly veiled sales call. Give away a dinner for two at a popular local restaurant or two free movie tickets to an upcoming popular movie. Everyone likes to eat out or see a good movie.

Of course you want to gain permission from the event organizer to give away the door prize. The only thing you ask in return is to place a small display stand with the promotion advertised on it along with a basket to capture people's cards. You might say something like "Win an all expenses paid dinner for two at the All Seasons Restaurant - compliments of <Your Name> and <Your Company>. Place your business card in this basket to win. Winner will be announced at the end of the meeting."

Here are a couple of things to consider. First, don't combine your cards with the event organizer's cards or door prize offers. The purpose of the promotion is to leave with your own set of business cards. And second, if possible incorporate the awarding of the door prize into the event. On an index card write out exactly what you want the president to say when awarding the door prize. You might say, *"On behalf of <Your Name> and <Your Company>, the winner of the Dinner for Two at the All Seasons Restaurant is..."* Ideally you should be standing near the president with your basket of cards. Allow the president or guest speaker to pick a name from the basket and announce the winner. Have the certificate in hand and present it to the winner in front of the attendees.

Clarify and Confirm

The last thing you want to do when meeting someone for the first time, no matter how unqualified he may be, is to reject, ignore or disagree with his or her comments. In situations like these, it is important to employ your best interpersonal skills and tactfully handle the prospect. Yes, you could just walk away, but assuming that's what most people do — including your competition — why not take advantage of the potential business to be gained.

A good rule of thumb anytime you have the tendency to reject, ignore or disagree with anything someone else is saying to you, is to simply clarify and/or confirm the statement. Find out *why* the person feels or thinks the way they do by asking questions rather than immediately passing judgement. If you think you have a genuine understanding of why the person thinks or feels the way they do, *confirm* your understanding.

The use of these two simple skills will illustrate your listening skills, show the prospect you genuinely understand their concern and highlight your consultative approach to working with people.

Constructive Feedback

When warranted, you may want to offer some constructive feedback to others to help improve their overall presentation and networking skills. Stick with the obvious flaws and always ask permission from the person before offering your insights. Areas that warrant constructive feedback include: lack of eye contact, folded arms, hands always in pockets, negative body language, and lackluster presentation skills.

Even if the person has a laundry list of bad traits, focus on only one or two. Too much criticism, too fast can be devastating to some people. Remember, your intent is to help not hurt.

Lead off by saying something like, *"I'm not a professional public speaker, but if you are interested I may be able to share some tips with you to make your networking skills even better, would you like to hear them?"*

Allow the person to answer yes or no. If they say no, move on. Don't convince them they need your insights. If they say yes, lead off by mentioning a few positive things about their networking abilities. Without the use of the word "but" or "however", start the next sentence with one or two things the person could do to improve. And finish off with a couple strategies they could implement to instill the change.

Do a Presentation/Spotlight

Many organizations will allow members to spotlight their goods and services at various networking events. If you belong to an organization that allows these kinds of presentations, by all means sign up to get yourself slated to speak. Putting yourself in front of 10, 50 or 500 people is one of the most effective ways to get your message out to the masses.

However, the time to begin preparing your presentation is now. You should have a 1 minute, 5 minute, 10 minute, 20 minute and 1 hour version of your presentation ready and available on a moment's notice. The time to create your presentation is not the night before it's due and you certainly never want to "wing it".

Because public speaking is an art as well as a skill, when you put on a good show, people will remember it for years. Do what you can to make your presentation interesting, informative and whenever possible interactive. The best networking presentations we have seen are the ones where the audience genuinely learns something new, sees and/or participates in some kind of demonstration and has fun while doing it. Liven up your presentation with everything from colorful hand-outs to sample products the audience can take home. Use colorful pictographs to illustrate numbers and use three dimensional props whenever possible.

Finally, offer a door prize to a member of the audience and a special offer unique to everyone in the room. As soon as you are done, get your name back on the list for the next presentation opportunity.

The two most critical aspects of successful presentations are planning and delivery. Planning includes understanding the audience, assessing its needs, establishing objectives to meet its needs, researching the topic, designing the presentation, and making sure the facilities are adequate for the presentation.

Ninety percent of the success of a presentation can be attributed to planning. To develop a successful plan you need to answer the following questions:

✓ Who are your participants? Do they share the same experiences?

✓ Do participants have knowledge or skills that pertain to the topic?

✓ How many participants will attend the presentation?

✓ What is the preferred learning style of the group?

✓ How much time will you have for the presentation?

✓ How will you open and close the presentation?

✓ How will you get and keep their attention?

✓ What questions will you ask? What questions will they ask?

✓ What notes, visuals and materials do you need?

Delivery includes the presenter's style and his or her ability to effectively use verbal and nonverbal communication, questioning and reinforcement, group interaction, and the appropriate dose of humor. Some guidelines to make your presentation a winner include:

✓ Be sure to tell your audience why your presentation is relevant to them.

✓ Do not tell jokes unless you are a great story-teller...and then make certain your story isn't offensive.

✓ Show enthusiasm. People are more convinced by the enthusiasm of your message than by the message itself.

Door Prizes

Door prizes are one of the easiest and yet, least used methods to obtain hundreds, even thousands of leads with little or no effort on your part. Just about every retail store will welcome the following promotion in their store. Tell the store owner that you would like to purchase a $25 gift certificate (could be more, could be less) every week and award it in the form of a door prize to one of her customers. What's in it for you? Well, first you have to pick a retail store where the store's customers are your customers. In other words, if you sell life insurance you may want to choose maternity clothing stores and other related baby retail stores. Why? Because many young couples typically do not consider purchasing life insurance until they have their first child. Therefore, the store's customers will probably be a great source of leads for your life insurance business.

It's genuinely a win-win situation. The customer voluntarily places their name, address and telephone number into a jar or box that has your name and the name of the baby store on it along with an explanation of the promotion. The customer wins because he will receive a $25 gift certificate; the store wins because the customer will have to return to the store to redeem the certificate buying $25 or more worth of new products; and you benefit because the store's customers fit your customer demographic and psychographic profile. Depending on the success rate you have with the leads, rather than make the offer a one-time drawing, make it a give-away if they agree to set an appointment with you.

Auto repair shops can do a co-promotion with fast change oil stores, a caterer can do a promotion with a florist, and a retail golf store can do a promotion with a golf pro. Don't be surprised if this technique alone introduces you to hundreds of new prospects each and every week.

The best door prizes are those that don't cost you anything. A restaurant will gladly donate a $30 gift certificate if the owner feels he will receive $50 or $100 worth of free advertising. To ensure the restaurant owner gets a return on investment, attach a copy of the restaurant's menu with every promo piece where the door prize will be awarded. Print the restaurant's name on the flyers, tickets, advertisements, etc. As a last resort give the restaurant a copy of the business cards (database) you collected to award the door prize.

Simply provide the business owner who donates the door prize double the value back in free advertising and you'll never run out of door prizes.

5 Cards Please

Often when a professional networker recommends another business person, they couple it with the person's business card. For those of you who participate in lead groups, you may want to keep a store of members' cards with you so when you make a referral, you can accompany it with the person's card.

When meeting someone who can be easily referred to others you come in contact with, ask for five of their cards. This allows one for your database file, one for your Rolodex and a few extras to give away to others who may be in need of their services.

When you ask for five cards, the person you are asking immediately thinks differently of you. They either think you are a card collector or you probably have three or four people to pass on their card. This not only differentiates you from the competition, but also illustrates to the new contact that you will genuinely do what you can to promote their business.

Be Conspicuous

Whenever possible, sit, stand or position yourself in a conspicuous place. The front seat, a seat at the president's table or a seat at the guest of honor's table are all high visibility spots. Check with the meeting organizers and confirm what seats are available or which tables are typically used by the president and guest speaker.

If a networking reception precedes the luncheon or dinner, scout out a seat and mark it reserved by placing your purse, drink, literature, or anything that will signal to others the seat is saved. You may want to tip the chair up against the table, drink half the water and place the glass at the center of the place setting, or rumple up the napkin and lay it across the place setting.

If you are traveling in an airplane, the best seat location is the aisle seat. This gives you an opportunity to talk to everyone around you. Although most people may want to be left alone, some are looking for opportunities to socialize and network. The best part of networking on a plane is that no one is going anywhere for two or three hours and you have a great opportunity to develop a relationship.

When you are at cafeterias, meetings or club events, whenever possible sit with strangers. Although it may feel more comfortable to sit with friends you are missing out on golden opportunities.

When you are at a party, don't just eat the food and look at your plate; keep your chin up and look at people. Play the host. Introduce yourself to everyone around you. In fact, at every event you go to there are many people just standing around by themselves dying for someone to talk to them and take them out of this uncomfortable situation.

1 a Week for 5

Certain members of a group will be better lead sources than others. For example, common sense says that a mortgage broker will have a greater chance of obtaining leads from a residential real estate agent than a florist or printer. If there are certain businesses that are great sources of leads for your business, it is in your best interest to cultivate as many relationships with these kinds of key contacts as possible.

One way to establish a strong business referral relationship is to offer the key contact a lead a week for the next five weeks. Don't brag. Don't insist on speaking with the contact each time you call. If anything, act nonchalantly about the leads you provide.

At the same time, you do want to keep in touch with the contact on a business-personal level. Send the person a literature pack on you and your company. If you are driving by the contact's office, stop in and say hello. The key is to maintain a presence, but not become a pest.

Do your best to use high quality hot leads. Once the key contact lands a sale or two, you will then have an "in" to sell your services. They'll owe you one, or two or three.

Exploit Your Competition's Weaknesses

Do you ever feel your competition has 99.9% of the market and you have none? One way to penetrate the competition's stronghold on your prospects is to exploit a weakness. Find an area of dissatisfaction or a segment of the business where you can make a far better offer than your competition. Are they slow to answer the phone? Are their prices higher than yours? Do they offer a money back guarantee? Do they offer volume discounts?

When introducing yourself to others, incorporate your key strength into your introduction. You might say, *"Hello, my name is Joe Smith and I am with ABC Company. We help businesses reduce by 50% the time and expense associated with their office supplies. Our prices average 25% below retail and we offer same day delivery. Consequently, our customers can focus on their business and not have to worry about shopping for the best price and waiting for supplies to be delivered."*

Guest Speaking — Anytime, Anywhere

Guest speaking is one of the best ways to get your name in front of the masses and at the same time establish trust, authority and credibility. Like any presentation, you want to be well prepared and incorporate as much impact into your presentation as possible. Whenever possible, use visual aids such as props, charts, graphs, hand-outs, and demonstrations.

If you are not a seasoned speaker, before jumping too fast into the public speaking arena, you may want to take a couple of speaking courses or join an organization like Toastmasters (1-800-9-WE-SPEAK). Just as public speaking will allow you to reach tens or hundreds of people in one sitting with the benefits of using your product or service, if your speaking ability is not up to par, it could give that same number of people a reason *not* to do business with you. Practice, practice and practice your presentation. Allow others to provide you with objective feedback and always be willing to look for areas of improvement.

One of the best ways to enter the guest speaking market is by letting others know you are available to speak. Start with small groups and work your way up to larger groups. For most speakers, the speech will be an unpaid event. However, if you get good at what you do and your topic is in demand by enough people, you may find you are able to charge a fee for your services. A great place to start is non-profit organizations that have a need for your services.

One of the best strategies to get people to invite you to speak is to make your presentation focus on a generic topic. No one wants to hear a 20 minute or one hour advertisement for your product or service. Speak on a topic related to your industry. Accountants can speak on any tax law changes or how to maximize business deductions without being audited. A stock broker can review an investing philosophy or 10 proven investing techniques, etc.

The power behind a presentation is that an audience member will be impressed by your knowledge and presentation skills; that well earned goodwill will transfer into sales leads.

Handshake

What do you give people you meet even more than your business card? Your hand. American business culture states that when you meet someone for the first time and you are within a few feet of that person, a handshake is expected. Whether you are a man or a woman, important or unimportant, young or old, a handshake is one way to greet those you meet for the first time and those you meet on a regular basis.

If you are confident you have a good firm handshake, then you can probably skip this chapter. But for those of you who aren't so sure or know someone with a weak handshake, read on. What is the use of dressing professionally, arriving on time and doing all the other right things if you begin or end the interaction with a limp, clammy handshake.

Everything you do must be congruent with the message you wish to send. One item out of place puts a crack in the facade and creates hesitation in those who meet you for the first time.

To ensure that you have a good, firm, business-like handshake complete the following exercise. Get yourself 10 small index cards or pieces of paper. As you come across people you already know — ideally business associates or coworkers — let them know you are doing a handshake experiment. Tell them it will take all of 30 seconds and the data they give you will be invaluable. Tell them in a moment you are going to shake their hand like you would normally shake hands with someone you are are meeting for the first time. Ask them to rate the handshake on a scale of 1 to 10, with 10 being the best handshake possible. Tell them you will be asking 10 other people for this information and that their responses will be anonymous. In other words, after the handshake and when you collect the data, you will not look at it until all 10 handshakes have been completed. Let the participant know, that in addition to their number, especially if it is a low number, to feel free to identify what was wrong with the shake or what you can do to improve it. After you receive your 10 data inputs, review the data and see where you fail. If you are in the 8 to 10 category, keep doing what you are doing. If you are in the 5 to 7 category, look for some insight as to how to improve your handshake. If you are in the 1 to 5 category, do not shake hands with another business contact until you correct what is wrong.

For most people, the problem is that their handshake is not firm enough. When you shake a hand, hold on for a second or two. Make the initial grasp slightly harder than the person's hand you are shaking. Now if they have a death grip, don't give them one back...but stay firm during the entire painful ordeal. If your grip is too strong, lighten up a little.

If you suffer from clammy, sweaty hands, before you walk into a networking event, rub a powder type antiperspirant on your hands. By the way, for those of you who have sweaty feet, this trick works on feet too.

To Refer or Not to Refer

Don't fall into the referral trap and refer your friends and hard earned clients unless you feel confident and have proof they can deliver the goods and services they promise. Unfortunately, we have learned this lesson the hard way. When you refer one person to another, not only is the recipient of the referral's reputation on the line, but more importantly so is yours. You work at establishing trust and rapport with your customers and over time you become viewed as a resource in people's minds. When they need a recommendation, they call you because of the time and effort you have invested in making contacts and building relationships with hundreds, even thousands of business owners. One bad referral can literally remove all credibility you have with that person and all future recommendations and requests you make may be tainted.

When you first begin to extensively network you begin to apply the key concept of successful business networking: *you have to give business to get business.* Also as a professional, you realize you personally can only give so much business. After all how many houses, mortgages, life insurance policies, cars, etc., can you buy in a year? In order to give business on a grand scale, you are going to be in a position where you are going to give your business contacts to other people who you know that are in the market for homes, mortgages, life insurance policies, etc. Because you are closest to your friends and existing customers, many of these referrals will consist of their needs. The last thing you want to do is recommend anyone who is going to make you look bad. As a matter of fact, you should only pass leads to those networking contacts you either have had personal dealings with or know first hand of people who have. Their reputations should be spotless and they should have a genuine business philosophy that places the customer's needs first and foremost above their own.

However, even under the best of circumstances things can go wrong you can be blamed for the recommendation. One way to reduce dramatically this "backfire" effect is to recommend a minimum of three contacts that could satisfy the customer's need. Suggest, preferably in writing, that they contact, interview and obtain information on all three. And only after they have had a chance to review carefully each prospective vendor, should they come to their own conclusion.

Don't be to eager to recommend the products or services of those people you have only met once or twice for a short period of time at a networking event. Successful networking is based on relationships, trust and mutual consideration. You want to pass leads to other business people who will treat your customer with as much, if not more respect, than you show them. Be cautious and expand your contact base with care.

Hot Lead? Warm Lead? Cold Lead?

We are all salespeople. For some, it may be a title, for many it may be just one small part of your overall job description. The leads you pass to others will fall into a variety of categories. If you know of someone ready, willing and able to buy the product or service of a business associate of yours, for the most part you could define that as a *hot* lead. In other words, when your business associate contacts the motivated buyer a sale will be made. Maybe with him, maybe with one of his competitors, but the prospect may buy.

A *warm* lead is someone you pass to a business contact who has expressed a desire in the product or service your business contact offers. The sale will probably occur, but not immediately. Maybe with the right incentive, financing or questions being answered the sale will be made sooner than later.

Finally, a *cold* lead is one that you have no contact with the prospect. You know that the client currently uses the product or service your contact sells, and that there is a chance that rather than buy again from the competition, the prospect may buy from your contact.

So the question becomes: which of the above leads do you want people to pass to you? Personally, we'll take all of them. However, there are some people and some lead groups that consider a valid lead to be a hot lead only. If the lead you pass is "hot," the prospect is looking to buy immediately; be sure to indicate that in your contact. Let people know all the kinds of leads you look for to develop a prospect profile. There is nothing worse than sitting on a lead for a week only to contact the prospect and learn of a $50,000 purchase made the day before.

Even if you can't do anything with the lead now — in the meantime leverage the lead *(see Leveraging Your Leads)* with another networker or two.

60 Second Commercial

Many networking events will provide you with an opportunity to introduce yourself to the group at hand. Typically, no more than a minute is allotted for such introductions so you will want to maximize the 60 seconds you have available to you. Although there is a lot you can do in 60 seconds, you will want to include certain critical information.

Key components of an introduction include:

✓ Your name

✓ Your company

✓ A memory hook

✓ A general benefit statement

✓ An attention getter

✓ What constitutes the kind of customers you are looking for

Other components you may want to include are:

✓ Your title

✓ Your address/location

✓ Any special offers to the group

✓ A quick demonstration

✓ Your 800 number/phone number

An example of an effective 60 second introduction you might use if you were a residential real estate agent might be:

Did you know that there are 5 improvements for under $100 you can make to your home that will increase its value up to $5,000. Good morning, my name is Joe Smith and I'm with ABC Realty. For over 10 years we have been successful at getting sellers top dollar for their homes. If you, or anyone you know, would like to learn how your home could sell for up to 10% more than your neighbor's, give me a call and I'll send you a free Strategic Sellers Report. And remember what they say, "if you don't sell it with ABC, you'll be out some dough-ray-me." Again, my name is Joe Smith with ABC Realty.

If possible in your sixty-second commercial always focus on who you are talking to and the benefits that are important to them. In other words, your introduction should state how you or your company can help him and/or his networking group save, gain or accomplish something.

The Lead Bank

In the networking arena there is something called the proverbial lead bank. This bank keeps track of the leads you put in and the leads you take out. Unfortunately, the bank rarely pays any interest and as a matter of fact you often will have to invest up to three times what you ever get to withdraw. Why bank at the lead bank? Because it's the only bank in town.

When you first start to network, you will be disappointed real fast if you expect a 1 to 1 return on the leads you invest. When you first start, you should expect that for every five leads you invest, you will only receive one back in return. In other words, you might invest 14 leads and receive nothing and when you deposit your fifteenth, you finally get back three.

The reason why the return is so low is the bank works in theory and if that wasn't bad enough it also works on the honor system. In theory, for every lead you invest you get one in return. Also, theory states a lead is a lead. But odds are you may only know one or two of the people who are going to be buying or selling a house this week whereas you probably know 30 or 40 who plan to send flowers on Mother's Day. Consequently, the florist, on a lead for lead basis, has more withdrawals than the real estate agent. The honor system says that for every lead you get you should invest a new lead into the bank. It only takes a few people to take leads from the bank and not invest leads to throw off the bank deposit and withdrawal ratios. However, look on the bright side. Although, the florist may make 50+ withdrawals a year from the lead bank and the real estate agent only three or four, the income generated for the real estate agent may be 20 times that of the florist.

Quality, not just quantity, is the key to investing in leads. However, a general rule of thumb states that the more leads you invest in others, the more likely you will have leads returned to you.

Leverage Your Leads

The use of this technique alone could double or triple your referral business in a matter of weeks. Even savvy business people who have been successfully networking for years rarely employ this secret and very successful technique. Most business people we know tend to develop relationships with a limited number of business people in various professions. They tend to cultivate and pass leads to one stockbroker they know, or one real estate agent they know or one florist they know. As a result, the amount of leads they will receive (or are owed) from these people will be in a one-to-one ratio. For example, if you know someone who wants to sell their house you pass that info to a real estate contact. In theory, that real estate person now owes you a lead.

However, the key to maximizing the number of leads you receive can be easily doubled or tripled overnight through the concept of leverage. Rather than pass that real estate lead to one real estate contact you have, pass it to three. If you do not have three real estate contacts, being in possession of a hot lead is a great way to introduce yourself and your company. Ask a business associate to give you the names of a couple of agents they know to be competent. The information they provide to you is in turn a lead they can pass to their real estate friend.

By leveraging each lead you receive into two or three leads, instead of one favor being owed to you, you now have three. Remember, most professional salespeople are only interested in the lead itself. If it doesn't pan out, that is their problem. However, they will still want to keep you on the lookout for them and the way to do that is to pass you leads of people they know who are interested in your product or services.

This approach also has a couple of ancillary benefits built into it. First, it makes you look good almost all of the time. It is not uncommon to tout the benefits, experience and responsiveness of a business contact, only to pass the lead and for whatever reason, that person never contacts your lead source. Shame on that business person, but more importantly it makes you look bad in your contact's eyes. By passing the lead to three people, you can be assured that one, two or maybe all three will contact the person. Now, the contact is impressed with the calls — and you look good.

The second benefit is that it eliminates the need for you to recommend any one individual. Take it from first hand experience, the last thing you need is to recommend someone to one of your contacts and the person turns out to be a flop. Bad service, inferior products or just unprofessional behavior in general can all be reasons why a contact would end up blaming you for their bad dealings. Again, by recommending three, you leave it up to the prospect to choose among competing businesses. Should the transaction go sour, you are far less likely to be blamed for the outcome.

Finally, this technique also has a drawback. You may decide it is in your best interest not to leverage many of your leads. If you have developed a lucrative networking relationship with certain contacts, where you provide them with leads that turn into sales and they provide you with leads that turn into sales, don't rock the boat. If those contacts find out you have been passing leads to their competitors, while they have been exclusively passing leads to you, the risk of alienating these valuable networking contacts is high. Check the policies of your lead groups and adhere to the rules that govern passing leads outside the group.

Listening Skills

A professional networker has expert listening skills. You have two ears and one mouth and they should be used proportionately during any networking interaction. Listen to what the person is saying. Listen to everything the person is saying. Remember, as a professional networker you are not only listening for opportunities for the products and services you sell, but for the products and services of the 200 or 300 contacts you have in your networking portfolio.

The goal for everyone is to become active listeners. You can be an active listener by following these guidelines:

✓ Limit your own talking.

✓ Concentrate on the person.

✓ Don't interrupt.

✓ Paraphrase what has been said.

✓ Talk in a conducive setting.

✓ Be interested and show it.

✓ See things from their viewpoint.

✓ Notice nonverbal communication.

✓ Turn off your worries.

✓ Don't prejudge.

✓ Don't rush the other person.

Rarely will we meet someone and not walk away with some nugget of information that can be parlayed into a lead for two or three people. Often one person, may have multiple needs. Consequently, one interaction can generate into 3 prospect needs, which in turn can be leveraged into at least six and probably nine leads. Combine that with the fact that during an average one-hour long networking function you can meet 30 new people and could walk away with over 100 leads! Even if not one of those leads is for you, if you apply the 5 to 1 principle it could result in 20 leads returned to you over the next couple of months.

People like to complain. They often will share their problems or tell success stories, all of which are chock full of business opportunities if you know how to listen. For example, when a prospect says, *"Business is so good, we are in the process of formulating a plan to hire three new salespeople."* — that's a potential lead for a management and recruiting firm (to go out and find the person); a temporary employment agency (to temporarily fill the position or possible secretarial support for the three new salespeople); a sales training company (to train the reps); a management consultant (to train the managers to help manage growth); a commercial real estate firm (possible new or larger office space is required); a printer (new business cards, announcements).

One of the key benefits of networking is putting to good use and making profitable the information you obtain from others in your daily interactions. From this point forward, if you use your listening skills wisely, rarely is your interaction with anyone a waste of time. Think big, you not only are the sales arm of your company, but also the sales arm of 200 or 300 other businesses. The nice part about this relationship, is that if you choose your networking contacts wisely, you too will now have 200 or 300 salespeople out in the field working for you.

Look Important, Act Important and Feel Important

It's usually pretty easy to spot the unsuccessful business people in a room at a networking event. It's even easier to spot the successful people in a networking event. What's the difference? The unsuccessful people are usually: the shy ones; sitting; talking to no one; checking their watch; with a plate of hors d'oeuvres; reading their own sales literature; talking to the waiters or waitresses; inappropriately dressed; need a haircut; unpolished shoes; polyester pants; knit tie (or worse, clip-on tie); frayed suit or shirt collars, etc.

The successful people on the other hand are typically the ones who are: dressed sharp; neat; clean; well tailored suit; silk tie; starched, crisp, white shirt; nice polished shoes; always talking to someone, usually two or three people; always the last to sit down; neatly groomed; ready with a firm handshake for everyone they meet, etc.

As a networker, you want to make sure you meet and get to know both of these people. However, as a role model you will want to emulate the second person, not the first. Visuals are very important. The descriptions of the two people outlined above denote certain images in your mind about the type of people these people actually are. They are not based in reality, but based on stereotypes. But let me ask you a quick question, if you could only go on looks, mannerisms and gut feel, who would you want to sell your house? Remove one of your kidneys? Prepare your business financial plan? Represent you in court?

If you look important and act important, people will

perceive you as important. They will approach you and want to get to know you. You must exude confidence and success. One of the most inexpensive ways to do that when you are first starting or building a business is to look and act important. Don't let your clothes, your mannerisms or your attitude be the reason people pass you by at a networking event. And, for those of you who are in a so called "blue collar" profession, i.e., auto mechanics, carpenters and painters, following this advice will act like a magnet in attracting new business. How you look says a lot about how you work. Personally, if I needed someone to paint my house, work on my car or build a new deck on my house, give me a person who is neat, clean and shows attention to detail any day over a sloppy person with dirty fingernails.

Irresistible Offers

On occasion you will meet people who are currently in the market to buy the products and services you have to sell. Usually, they have already contacted the competition and plan to make a decision in the next few days. How will you trump the competition? Easy, make them an offer they can't refuse.

The time to create an irresistible offer is not while you are talking to the prospect. Doing so often leads to selling the farm to make the sale. In other words, you give so much away or discount your price, you leave little or no profit for yourself. You should always be armed with a few irresistible offers that will clinch the sale and leave your competition in the dust.

Make the offer unique, write it on the back of your business card and sign it. Have the prospect present it back to you at the time of sale or enclose it with payment in the invoice. The prospect should feel you are doing something special. If you pull out a stack of coupons, the prospect may think your offer is a gimmick available to anyone.

Of course what you offer will depend on your business. However, here are a few guidelines to keep in mind when creating one:

✓ Rather than discount your offer, add value. For example, if you sell copiers, include a free six month service contract valued at $150. Assuming your competition would charge the same amount for service, you sell the copier at full price and land the service contract at the same time. Meanwhile, your competitor is $150 more.

✓   Offer a two-for-one or buy two and get one free kind of deal. The key here is to move volume of your product.

✓   Bundle your product or services into a package. This technique will actually have the customer pay upwards of 50% more than anticipated, but because related items are being included, i.e., things the prospect will probably buy eventually, it's a good deal. For example, if you sell computers, bundle a bunch of software with it. If you are an accountant, offer a personal tax return with payment on the person's business tax return.

Having five or six irresistible preplanned and ready to go offers will allow you to not only walk away with a lot of leads from a networking event, but a couple of sales too. By making an interaction with you valuable, you can be assured a steady stream of referrals in the future.

Slogans

Here are some slogans that we've heard while networking:

Your Trash is Our Cash
— a cleaning company

Get Out of Town!
— but before you do, call me! — a travel agent

I'm the Guy with the Square Feet
— a commercial real estate agent

Our Minds are Always in the Gutter
— a gutter replacement contractor

You Can be a Filter or Buy a Filter
— a drinking water filter salesman

When meeting people for the first time, starting off your presentation or introduction with a catchy slogan can position your company in the person's mind for the rest of their life. Standing out from the competition is tough in today's marketplace. One easy and inexpensive way to do it is through the use of a slogan.

The best slogans rhyme, use a play on words, are funny, thought provoking, and should always relate to your business or you in some unique way. If you have a great slogan, you may want to carry it through to your business cards, letterhead, sales materials, company vehicles, advertising specialties, and of course your introductions. You may also want to trademark your slogan to prevent a competitor from stealing it.

Remembering Names

One of the biggest fears and embarrassments a networker can have is forgetting the name of a person you just met less than a minute ago. There are a variety of memory techniques and name games you can play with yourself, but here is a technique that is foolproof. When you meet with someone for the first time, one of the first things you should do is ask for their business card. If they do not have a card (shame on them), take out one of your own, scribble over your name and information so you don't get it confused with a fresh card and mistakenly hand it to someone else, and write their name, company name, phone and fax numbers on it. Once you have their card in hand, keep it there. Don't put it in your pocket, don't mix it with your cards, keep it in your hand or on top of the other cards from people you have met. As you speak to the person casually glance down at the card as needed to recall that person's name or to glean additional information about them or their company.

In the event the person does not have a card taking the extra effort to write down their information will illustrate your genuine interest in the prospect. In addition, you can bet that no one else will go to the trouble of doing so, thus minimizing the possibility of a competitor following up.

Meet, Greet, Trade & Aid

Maximizing the number of people you meet during a networking event depends on your approach to the interaction. A novice networker will arrive at an event and walk away with only one or two new contacts. Often they will spend 10 or 15 minutes talking with the same person thus reducing greatly the amount of time available to meet other contacts.

Meet, Greet, Trade & Aid is a system that will ensure the maximum number of new contacts are made with the greatest degree of personal impact on each contact. The following steps comprise the system:

✓ *Meet:* Approach a stranger in the room and introduce yourself to the person.

"*Hello, my name is Joe Smith.*"

✓ *Greet:* Greet the prospect by shaking hands or leaning forward slightly and ask for their name.

"*What is your name?*"

✓ *Trade:* Trade cards, pleasantries and obtain/provide background information.

"*It is a pleasure to meet you. Do you have a card? What do you do for a living?*"

Then probe to obtain background information about the prospect. Qualify the prospect for your business products or services or those of other contacts in your portfolio. Questions to do this include:

"*Do you currently use <Your> services/products?*"

"*How often, how much, how many, what dollar amount, etc.?*"

"Who is your current supplier/vendor?"

"What do you like best about them?"

"If you could change one thing about them, what would it be?"

Even, if you uncover an immediate need for your product or service, hold off on presenting it until you have Aided the prospect.

✓ *Aid:* You want to establish yourself as a resource, as a giver of business and not just another salesperson looking for a quick sale. The best way to position yourself and create this role is to Aid the prospect. To aid the prospect is to provide them with information that will further their business. Aid ideally is a hot lead, someone interested in purchasing their product or service immediately. However, Aid can also be a series of warm or information type leads. Maybe you know business owners whose customers would be ideal customers for this prospect *(see A Good Lead For Me Is)*. To begin the aid process you might say:

"Who are your typical customers?"

"What kind of business do you look for?"

"What areas are you looking to expand into?"

"What would be a good lead for you?"

Any or all of the above questions can be appropriate during your initial introduction. Once you have a clear understanding of the kinds of leads this person is looking for, Aid the prospect. Ideally, you could reach in your pocket and provide them with one or two business cards of hot leads. *(See Business Cards)* If not hot leads, at least provide them with the names (and business cards) of one or two business owners who might be a good lead source for them. And if you can't do that, provide them with the names of a couple of personal contacts you have that could use this person's product or service.

Only after you have AIDed the prospect should you return to the opportunity that exists for your business. The prospect will be receptive to your offer due to the fact you have just offered valuable information to him or her.

This system has taken years to perfect, but we find you can establish solid relationships on the principle that less is more. Imagine only spending a minute with someone and not only are you impressed by the way they look, act, speak, and conduct themselves but you also walk away with a couple of hot leads (and business cards) in your pocket all in less than 60 seconds. "Wow, that guy is amazing" or "I want to get to know this guy" is often the feedback we get from others when their friends meet us for the first time.

Not only will this approach result in the maximum number of business contacts, but it will also result in the greatest number of on the spot sales, leads and future referrals.

Positive Language

Professional networkers inspire confidence not only by the way they look and act, but also by the way they speak. Always speak positively. The glass is always half full and you know nothing but a "can-do" attitude. Always be on the look out for solutions. Professional networkers do not complain. They don't speak badly about others, and they even have a good word about their competition.

A professional networker uses a consultative approach when addressing the business concerns of others. Look for opportunities in even the worst situations. People, especially prospects and customers, look to you for reassurance that you can indeed solve their problems. Any hesitation, doubt and of course, negative language does nothing to further your image in the customer's mind. As a matter of fact, those who rarely use positive language, rarely generate business at networking events.

Networking Mega Mixer

One way to make yourself the focus of attention and get 100 or more people talking about you and your business is to host your own networking event. We call them Mega-Mixers. The key behind a successful Mega-Mixer is the number of people, good food and good sponsors. We have hosted a number of 100+ person Mega-Mixers and the total cost out of pocket was $0. The way to do this is to find sponsors willing to expose their goods and services to 100+ business owners and decision makers.

Guidelines to hosting a Networking Mega-Mixer include:

✓ Pick a date and time that will be convenient for most people to attend. Allow for weather, traffic, sporting events, holidays, and work schedules. We have found Spring and Fall to be the best seasons, and either Tuesday, Wednesday or Thursday evening from 5:30 to 7:30 PM to be best. Schedule the event at least 90 days ahead to allow for maximum word of mouth and advertising. Be careful not to pick the night of the World Series or the day before a holiday or the date another major business event traditionally is scheduled (i.e., a local Chamber of Commerce dinner, etc.)

✓ First find an area of your geographic region that will be convenient for most people to attend. If you have the facility to host 100 people in-house, then hold it at your place. Otherwise, find a restaurant, hotel or bar willing to co-sponsor the event. We usually will negotiate with the facility to co-sponsor. In exchange for getting 100+ people to show up at their restaurant and include the name of their facility in all the advertising and tickets we print, they must provide discounted drinks, i.e., $1 drafts, free soft drinks and free hors d'oeuvres.

Make sure you pick a location that can hold 100+ people and make sure it is reserved for you. Put your agreement with the restaurant/bar in writing. A cordial letter confirming what you are doing and what is expected of the facility is the best way to do it. Maintain contact with the facility co-sponsor on a regular basis until the night of the event. If possible, stay away from outdoor settings due to heat and the event of rain. Also, work with people who understand the concept of a "WIN-WIN" relationship. Many restaurant owners don't see the value of having 100 new prospects visit their restaurant. If you must, rent a hotel meeting facility, but one way to eliminate the room charge is to coincide the event with an existing restaurant or hotel happy hour. Often they will have the space, drink specials and free hors d'oeuvres already available.

✓ Print tickets to the event and pass them out to your existing customers with your compliments. Put a $10 price tag on the ticket and then buy a rubber stamp that reads "PREPAID - Compliments of <YOUR COM-PANY>." Give each person you meet four tickets and let them know they must confirm their attendance prior to the event. Print on the ticket, seating is limited you must confirm your attendance prior to the event. Even though there will be no "sitting" at the event, when people think they have to save a seat they will call, otherwise they won't. On the ticket also print your company name, address and phone number. Include the date, time and location of the event. On the back of the ticket, instruct the guest to either staple their business card or allow space for them to write their name, business name, address, phone, fax number, and possibly a few qualifying questions. Do you currently use XYZ products? Yes No. Get a local printer to print the tickets for free and include a space on the ticket for the printer to include his name and phone number.

For every 100 people you want to attend the event, distribute 200 to 400 tickets. If you do not have 200 or more customers, release the next batch of tickets to your prospects, and finally keep a 100 or so for yourself to give to people you meet. Know what the facility's capacity is and keep track of your reservations. Over book the event by as much as 15%, but don't go too far beyond that. You want people talking about the success of the event for the next 6 months, not complaining about it. If you are hosting the event at a restaurant, encourage the owner to offer a special to those who stay for dinner. The restaurant could pick up as many as 30% of the attendees if the right special is offered. Have them create and post some type of sign at the entrance to the networking event.

Also on the ticket, explain briefly the purpose of the event *"ABC COMPANY MEGA-MIXER. 100+ Prospects together in 1 room. Bring 100+ business cards and be ready to network. Door prizes. Complimentary drinks and hors d'oeuvres."* Providing this information on the ticket will explain the event to those who did not receive the ticket directly from you.

✓ Encourage your inner circle of business contacts (your clients) to provide door prizes. Again, those who understand marketing and win-win relationships will volunteer door prizes gladly. Always give the door prize contributors the name of the winner and depending on the size of the door prize, all the people who attended the event.

✓ Get there early and set up a table. Ideally you should

have one entrance and exit into the event and you should be positioned next to it to meet every person who walks through the door. Have someone collect the tickets of all those who attend. If someone does not have a ticket, make them complete a new one prior to entering. Have paper sticker type name badges available for those networking amateurs who show up without a professional badge.

✓ Personally, we like a 100% reception style event, In other words, no guest speakers and no speeches by you the host. The more you make the event appear non-commercial, the more credibility you gain. People appreciate you were not there to sell them something at every turn. Toward the end of the event, before people begin to leave, award the door prizes. Doing so will eliminate having to mail/ship the door prize to the winner after the event.

✓ When done right, those 100+ people who attend will make it a priority to attend future events. Limit the Mega-Mixers to 3 or 4 times per year to keep the event special. When meeting people for the first time, many times your reputation will proceed you and people will request that you put them on your mailing list.

✓ Have a banner made with your company name hanging prominently from a wall to be seen by all.

Take Me Out to the Ball Game...

**Join the Alexandria Business Exchange
Networking Group and the Prince William
Cannons for an afternoon of Summer fun!**

Hamburgers, Hot Dogs, Salads, Chips, Soft Drinks, Beer, and much, much more.

Seating at the Ball Park is Very Limited and will be Reserved Upon Payment.
    -- reserve early....they expect the game to sell-out!

When: June 22,   4 PM (Rain or Shine)
Who: You, Your Spouse, Friends, Kids, ...Everyone
Where: Joe and Tracy Ilvento's Home
4132 Widebranch Lane, Woodbridge, VA
        and then later at the stadium.

Ticket Cost: $7 per person -- the pre-game party is FREE compliments of the Business Exchange

Dress: Very Casual -- Shorts, Sun Glasses -- if you want, you can even soak in the Hot Tub for awhile

The Roster: We will gather at Joe's house at 4 PM and eat, drink and be merry until 6 PM. At 6:15 PM we will convoy over to the Prince William County Stadium Complex. The Game starts at 7 PM and will end around 10 PM. For those of you who can't stay for the game, don't hesitate to attend the FREE pre-game party!

Directions: 95 South to Exit 158 B/Prince William Parkway East. Go 2.2 miles and make left onto Minnieville Road. Go 2.2 miles and make left onto Cardinal Drive. Go 1.3 miles and make left onto Greenmount Drive. Go 1/2 mile and make first left onto Widebranch Lane...we are at 4132 Widebranch Lane. 703/730-0300

YES! Sign me up.

Please reserve _____ tickets for me at $7 per ticket. Enclosed is my check made out to The Business Exchange for $_____. I can't make the game but I do want to make the pre-game party.

Including myself, I will be bringing _____ guests. (so we know how much food to prepare)

Name: _____
Address: _____
City/State/Zip Code: _____
Home Phone: _____

Mail and make check payable to:
The Business Exchange
4132 Widebranch Lane
Woodbridge, VA 22193

MARKET MONTHLY
MEGA◆MIXER
August 14th

Last Mega-Mixer Was Sold Out!

Back By Popular Demand!

FREE to MMM Subscribers

❖ Only $8 to Non-Subscribers.

❖ Join 100+ Other Business Leaders for a Night of Networking and Fun!

❖ First 100 Reservations Receive a special report by *Guerrilla Marketing International.*

❖ Door Prizes!

❖ Seating is Limited and All Attendees Must be Pre-Registered to Attend.

❖ 100 Prospects in One Room!

❖ Bring 100+ Business Cards. Name Tags will be Available.

❖ Event to be held at **Papa Razzi** Restaurant at Bailey's Crossroads.

Note: If you would like a Free Ticket to this event and others like it in the future, complete and mail the attached subscription card with payment.

CALL 703/730-0300

Menu Ordering

We are amazed at the people who show up at a breakfast, lunch or dinner meeting and order meals inappro-
priate for conducting business. The guidelines that follow not only apply in networking settings but also face-
to-face, one-on-one type appointments you might set
with your prospects and customers.

Let's start with human nature. Some people feel the
one way to recoup the cost of an event, that includes a
meal, is to eat a large meal. If the event costs $25, they
order and eat $30 worth of food. If you fall into this cat-
egory, one way to change your perspective of these food
related networking events is to view the cost of the event
as strictly an admission fee to get through the front door
and to view the meal that comes with the event as an
option. Your focus should be 100% on the event, the
contacts and potential business that exists in the room
and not on whether or not you should order the veal or
the chicken.

Although some people at every networking event try
it, you cannot hold a business conversation with a mouth
full of soup, bread or mashed potatoes. You are either
networking or you are eating; it is difficult to do both at
the same time. The only thing you can do, professionally, when you have a mouth full of food is listen.
Therefore, if your prospect is eating, you can be talking
and they have no other choice but to listen.

If the event requires ordering off a menu, choose an
easy to eat meal. Stay away from soup, anything that is
sticky like syrup and pancakes or waffles, and anything
with sauces. For the most part, stay away from foods that
drip, stick, stain, or smell. If possible order an appetizer
as your main course. Not only is the portion usually
smaller, but often these foods can be eaten with your

hands or are already prepared into bite size pieces. What you eat is as much a reflection as the tie or shoes you choose to wear. Remember, perception is reality. Who do I want as my stock broker, the guy who eats a rich cheese laden piece of meat that will put him to sleep this afternoon or someone who eats an energetic, vitamin rich, light salad. Especially, if you are overweight, be careful of the image you project to those around you.

Again, just because it is in front of you doesn't mean you have to eat it. If you are being served a set menu and don't want it, simply tell the waiter or ask if you could substitute something for the item, for example a piece of melon or a fruit cup instead of soup.

Incentive Program

One quick way to develop a lead program is to compensate people for thinking of you. At a minimum, when you receive a lead from someone that results in a sale, you should send a hand written thank you note. If your profession allows, you may also want to send along a gift certificate for dinner for two to a local restaurant or movie tickets or both.

Rather than acting after the fact, you can actually advertise the fact that you pay for referrals. One way to do this is with a referral post card program. On one side of the card pre-print your name and address; on the other side of the card at the top write, "This card may be worth $100 cash to you." Provide the reader with details on how to obtain the $100. For example, do you know anyone who is getting married this year? If so, write their name, address and phone number below and if they order their wedding flowers from us, you will receive $100 cash. Have a few hundred of these cards made and pass them out to people you meet or mail them to your existing customers or contact base.

You will be surprised at the number of leads you will generate. When a sale does occur as a result of the lead card, have the person who sent you the lead drop by the shop. Have a photograph taken with you presenting $100 cash to the person. Have the photo enlarged and keep it in your shop and do the same for every card related sale. People who come into the shop like pictures and will inquire how they too can earn $100 cash. Soon, you will have numerous leads coming in on a weekly basis and assuming the average wedding order might be $1,000, a $100 is a small price to pay.

THIS CARD IS WORTH $100 TO YOU!

Welcome to **Applied Business Communications, Inc. FAST CASH program.**
Simply complete the information below and when the organization identified
completes their seminar, **ABC, Inc.** will mail directly to you, **$100 CASH.**

Company Name:_____

Contact:_____

Phone: (_____)_____ Best Time To Call: _____

Type of Business: _____

Number Of Employees: _____ Your Name: _____

Why You Think This Organization Needs **ABC** Training?_____

_____

_____

▲

Pick-Up Your Pace 25%

Did you ever hear of the adage that if you want some-thing done, assign the task to a busy person? We believe that to be true. Why? Successful people are busy people. They always have things to do and places to go. They do not waste time or idly sit around before or after meetings without a purpose. They set appointments, use a sched-uler or calendar and have an air about them that radiates success.

One way to incorporate this powerful nonverbal mes-sage into your day-to-day interactions with people is to pick up your pace. When meeting with customers and prospects, pick up your pace 10%, 25%, and for some of you slugs out there, by as much as 50%. Speak faster, move faster, breathe faster, react faster — do everything faster by 25% and you will soon notice a change in the way others perceive you.

Some people, when asked when a good time to meet is, say anytime. Anytime? Don't they have work to do? Don't they have customers? Is business that bad that their whole day is free and anytime is a good time to meet? Always schedule your meetings, even if your whole day is free.

Power Contacts

One of the most important things you can do is develop a network of power contacts. These are people who are in a position to refer to you the exact kind of business you need. Real estate agents are good power contacts for mortgage brokers. General contractors are good power contacts for plumbers and electricians. Commercial leasing agents are good power contacts for moving companies, telephone hardware companies, office furniture companies, etc.

In other words, these people work in businesses that are compatible with yours. If a person buys a house, odds are they will need a mortgage. If they sign a new office lease for space across town, odds are they will need a mover or a new phone system. Creating a network of contacts whose business may precede yours will create an endless flow of hot, qualified leads.

Pay Attention/Show Respect

Remember being a great networker means that you lead by example. Just as you have earned the respect of your peers, you should show that same respect to them. One major dilemma that exists when you become a professional networker is that a lot of people will want to talk with you. Unfortunately, they will attempt to do this when others are speaking or making a formal presentation to an audience.

It is at times like these that you must lead by example. Because most speakers or presenters at a networking event are not professional speakers, they can easily become distracted by even the smallest interruption. If someone tries to speak with you while another is speaking, either write on a piece of paper, *"We'll talk after the presentation"* or quickly say, *"We'll talk after the presentation."* Even though you were not the one to spark up the conversation, the speaker as well as those around will become distracted and ultimately you will lose the respect of the group.

Paying attention to those just starting out is a great non-verbal technique that can reap huge benefits with regards to relationships and lead sharing. Rarely will someone approach newcomers to the group and show immediate interest in them and their products, especially if an existing member of the group already sells similar products or services. People become territorial; they view this new person as an outsider and as someone who must earn the right of passage into the group. Usually this right of passage is rooted in attendance, because existing group members don't know if you are a "one time visitor" to the group or are sincerely interested in becoming are part of it.

However, a professional networker who understands these "new person-visitor dynamics" can capitalize on the situation in almost every case. Seek out these people, befriend them and encourage their efforts. If you are the first, and often the only one to do this, they will be forever indebted to you. In addition, as a way of returning the favor, they may invite you to a meeting that they regularly attend. You will be surprised at who they might know. They may be the president of another lead group or organization and they in turn may invite you to one of their meetings. This isn't just wishful thinking — it works and we benefit from this kind of respectful relationship building all the time.

Get Published

Getting yourself published in local, regional or national newspapers, magazines and newsletters is a great way to keep your name in front of thousands of prospects. Almost regardless of the publication, most people will view you as an authority figure in your profession when your name is in print.

Whether you write articles, pose for photo opportunities or are quoted, getting yourself into print impacts those who see the print communication. Plus, through the power of reprints, you can use the article for years to come.

Quality vs. Quantity

Why is it better to give one hot lead a month to a person, than to give 10 cold leads. Because it can develop into a relationship like the boy who cried wolf. For example, if you receive four bad leads from someone chances are you're not motivated to follow-up on the fifth lead which is the big account you've been waiting for. A good networker passes on quality leads, and in turn expects to receive quality leads.

Make sure your leads are always warm. If possible, call the leads whose names you are giving out and tell them you know of somebody they should meet. By putting your reputation and credibility on the line you are giving a third party endorsement that is much more effective than just giving someone a name and phone number. In fact, when someone gives you a lead ask them if they will call for you, or set up a meeting.

Too many times we get everyone's business card without thoroughly knowing what they do, what they want, what their needs are, or how they can help us. Jot down on each card specific information to help you jog your memory.

Remember, you can't be everything to everybody and once you focus on what you really want fewer leads will give you better results.

Screen Groups

Before giving any presentation or going to any networking group, do your homework. Always ask yourself the following questions:

✓ Who are your participants?

✓ Do they share the same experiences?

✓ Do the participants have the knowledge or skills that pertain to the topic?

✓ What is their education level?

✓ How many participants will attend the presentation?

✓ What is the preferred learning style of the group (i.e., lectures, demonstrations)?

✓ How much time will you have for the presentation?

✓ How will you get and keep their attention?

✓ What questions will you ask?

✓ What questions will they ask?

✓ What notes, visuals and materials will you need?

Sitting Strategy

Do you ever notice the same people sit in the same places at each networking event? If you are given the opportunity to sit at an event, use a little sitting strategy. Use the opportunity to sit next to someone you have never met before or someone that you would like to get to know better. If you are a stranger to the group and the group is under 20 members, befriend one of the attendees and ask for the titles of the attendees and the names of the companies they represent. If the group is larger than 20 or time is short, have one of the members point out any power contacts *(see Power Contacts)* in the group. Just before the group sits down, stick near your power contact and do your best to sit next to the power contact or at least at the same table.

Often, you will have an opportunity to trade cards and introduce yourself sometime during the event. At a minimum, strike up a social conversation and say that you would like to get to know the person better after the event. Make arrangements to get in touch with the prospect after the event. Sometimes not getting a chance to introduce yourself and trade cards makes the contact and post-contact even stronger. Remember you know who the person is, but he or she doesn't know who you are. When the time comes to follow up, it will be no coincidence that you will have something in common and no coincidence that you sat next together at the event.

A Smile Attracts Conversation

Don't forget to smile! One of the best things you can do to attract conversation and contacts is to smile. Look approachable and friendly. Sometimes we get so focused on business and making the right contacts you forget to have fun. Smile, laugh and show a little of your personality to those around you.

Practice standing in front of a full length mirror. How do you look to others standing across the room? Do you look happy? Sad? Friendly? Unfriendly? Do you have a good side or a bad side? One way to keep a smile on your face during the whole event is to simply imagine everyone nude and the only one who is dressed is you. Smile and have fun.

In fact, smiling is so important that if you interview for a job with one major hotel chain and you don't smile at least five times in five minutes, there is no way you will ever get a job there.

Special Offer to Group

One thing you can offer the groups you attend is the right to ask you questions free of charge. This is a great way to obtain potential leads if you are an attorney, accountant or doctor. Making the offer to the group and their friends will help increase the likelihood they will call you rather than your competition for an answer to a question, especially if your competition charges for similar information.

You can offer a variety of freebies, discounts, specials and packages to group members.

Stay Late

Professional networkers know that just because the meeting ends that the opportunity to network doesn't. Good networkers not only arrive to an event early, but also stay late whenever possible. The idea is to maximize your time and effort at the event. You can maximize your time after the event by:

✓ Finishing any unfinished conversations you started earlier.

✓ Meeting with group members immediately after the event.

✓ During the event set appointments for after the event.

✓ Use this time to approach those people you did not get a chance to meet earlier.

✓ Casually walk out the door exchanging greetings and business cards.

Just because the event is over doesn't mean you have to stop networking.

Strangers Only

Your policy in meeting and speaking with people at any event is to speak with strangers only. In other words, don't fall into your comfort zone and begin a conversation with those in the room you already know. Remember, act as if you own the place *(see Act Like You Own The Place)* and as if you were the host and not the guest. Approach people and simply introduce yourself. Only after you have met every stranger in the room should you permit yourself the luxury of conversing with people you do know.

Testimonials

Have you done business for someone in the group? Were they happy? Did they give you a verbal compliment? In addition to asking that they put the compliment in writing, you should ask them to thank you publicly in front of the group. This is the best form of advertising you can get in a group setting. One of the benefits of this kind of public compliment is that it is often contagious. Usually, once one person stands up with a testimonial, others who have used your service will add to the public compliments and offer their stories and experiences too.

When you are fortunate enough to get this kind of positive exposure, be sure to thank the member(s) who complimented you. If appropriate at a future meeting, not the same meeting, compliment those who have complimented you in the past.

If you don't have a customer in the group, one technique to vary your handout is to pass out copies of a testimonial letter you received from a client. *(see Hand Outs)*

Track Leads

If you are a member of a lead group *(see Lead Groups)* or the president, a great way to ensure that everyone is contributing to the group is to track the leads passed by each member. The best way to illustrate the numbers is through a graph. On the left side of the page identify each member by name and rank them by the number of leads passed to date. Depending on the number of times you meet per year, you should restart the graph every month or 5 meetings. If you can also chart on a separate graph leads year-to-date.

Those who do not produce leads should be dropped from the lead group and replaced with another person who is willing to participate. It is in the group's best interest to consist of productive members only.

Reverse Networking: Trade Shows

Your participation in a trade show should be viewed simply as reverse networking. Rather than you approaching every stranger, every stranger will approach you. Make sure you develop a 60 second presentation that is quick and to the point to determine interest among booth visitors.

Qualify your prospects by finding out the following:

✓ Can they afford your product or service?

✓ Can the prospect influence the purchase?

✓ Is there a need for your product or service?

✓ Determine the visitor's place in the buying cycle.

✓ Establish the date of application or purchase.

✓ Be aware of body language.

While speaking to those who visit your trade show booth:

✓ Probe and interview for buying cues. Listen for cues like "when" can I order this or "can" I get it in a color.

✓ Record information about the potential prospect and get a business card. Write any additional information about the prospect on the business card.

✓ Be proactive. Don't just sit in your booth — interact with people who pass. You will miss a lot of opportunities if you wait for people to stop and ask questions.

✓ Give immediate attention to people coming into your booth. Trade show attendees hate to wait.

✓ Don't allow your time to be monopolized by any one booth visitor. Unless it is a big sale you plan to close that moment, delay the formal presentation and small talk until after the show. *(see Meet, Greet, Trade & Aid)*

Your networking doesn't stop when the trade show is over. It's vital that you follow-up after the show. This is the biggest mistake many exhibitors make. They fail to follow-up.

Trade Show Marketing Blitz

If you are attending a trade show make it a point to collect a card from *every* trade show booth participant. Why pick up the cards of people you would never do business with? Easy, use them as leads to pass to those you know who could do business with them. You could sweep an entire trade show in about an hour. No small talk, no introductions, just get a card and move on to the next booth. They are paying good money to sell to those in attendance and the last thing they want to hear is your presentation to them. Enter the names into a database *(see Business Card Database)* and follow up with direct mail, a cold call, Mega Mixer *(see Networking Mega Mixer)* or telemarketing program.

Visuals are Great

Stop talking and pull out the pictures. If you have a business that lends itself to visual support, don't miss using this valuable opportunity as often as possible. Before and after photos, charts, graphs, and picto-grams are effective ways to visually represent your product or service to others.

I once met a woman who baked elaborate cakes. She converted her business card into an effective visual sales tool. On one side she had the standard business card information, name, business name, title, phone, fax, etc., and on the other side was a full color picture of one of her cakes. Her card actually was a reprinted photo and her business card information was a label stuck to the back. If your budget allows, you can even have photo cards made professionally. The photo was so effective and her work so professional that I still have the card today. The night I met this woman, I was so impressed with her work that I showed her card to three other people. Without the photo, her card would have been mixed with all the others and the fact that she was an extraordinary cake maker would have gone unnoticed.

Whenever you have a chance to illustrate your business, a feature, a benefit, a happy customer using your product use it. Make it a hand out, laminate it and pass it around for others to see. Blow it up to poster size and post it on a wall. Do whatever it takes to get it noticed by others.

One way to use visuals effectively is to customize an item that you can get into the hands of potential clients. An advertising specialties company offers items like pens, rulers, booklets, calendars, magnets, and many more items that you can customize with your name, telephone number, logo, picture, etc.

Vertical Networking

Vertical networking is probably one of the easiest, yet least used techniques to build a multitude of prospects in a specific market area. Whereas most people if asked will not be able to think of someone who needs your product or service right now, if you ask them for the name of their accountant, dentist or insurance agent, they can rattle those names off with ease.

A vertical market is one that focuses on a single common denominator as a prospect qualifier. You can choose titles, geographic area, income level, number of children, etc. So rather than say you are looking for prospects who have a need for your product or service, knowing that your product or service appeals to people who have children, you might simply ask a contact for the names of people who have children.

Let's assume you sell life insurance. Everyone knows someone who has children; whereas if you asked for the names of people who are in the market to buy life insurance, not many people could give you an answer. Because you know that people with children are more likely to buy life insurance, you use this vertical market as the basis to obtain prospects. Ideally, you develop a custom direct mail piece that speaks to families with children and a custom sales presentation with children as the focus.

One month you may decide to go after families with children, the next month accountants, the next month stock brokers. Each time you select a different vertical market, revise your direct mail materials and sales presentation to appeal to that vertical market. Your ability to obtain leads will be easier than ever before. Rather than looking for hot leads you simply want the names of people your friends and associates do business with.

Understand that your closing percentages will be lower, however, you will begin to develop a strategic marketing database that you will be able to use for years to come.

Leveraging Questions for Any Networking Event

Many business people squander networking opportunities by incessantly talking about themselves. Successful networking requires that you get out of your mind and into the mind of the person you are talking to by asking the right questions. The following queries can lead you to what you want:

✓ Can you introduce me to?

✓ Who else should I read, go to or do?

✓ Who has made a difference in your life lately?

✓ How else can I assist you?

✓ What do you recommend regarding? (i.e., getting clients)

✓ What insiders' report or newsletters do you receive?

✓ Who else should I meet?

✓ How can we take what we've done and use it again?

✓ What do I need to do to make something happen?

✓ Who makes the decisions?

It's Not What You Say — But How You Say It

Only 7% of the messages people perceive are through the words you use. Another 38% come through the tone of your voice and 55% are communicated through your body language. To enhance how you come across and how you are perceived by others, follow these golden rules:

✓ Use good eye contact — Focus on the person you're talking to. Nothing establishes rapport better than good eye contact.

✓ Smile — People would much rather deal with someone who is upbeat and happy than someone who is dour.

✓ Be enthusiastic — People are more convinced by your enthusiasm than by anything else.

✓ Use humor — Humor makes you more likable. Also people will remember you and what you're saying.

✓ Use stories and anecdotes — Create mental pictures. The more you can create a picture in someone's mind, the easier it is to persuade him or her to your way of thinking.

Be Memorable

To become successful you must make yourself memorable. You want people to think about you when opportunities come up. There are a variety of ways to become memorable such as:

✓ The first to say hello.

✓ Introduce yourself to others.

✓ Take risks. Don't anticipate rejection.

✓ Display your sense of humor.

✓ Make an extra effort to remember people's names.

✓ Give your word, then keep it.

✓ Have humility.

✓ Show curiosity and interest in others.

✓ Tell others about important events in your life.

✓ Communicate enthusiasm and excitement about things and life to others.

✓ Be able to tell about what you do in a few short sentences.

✓ Use eye contact and smile at your first contact.

✓ Seek common interests, goals and experiences.

✓ Keep abreast of current events.

✓ Express your feelings, opinions and emotions.

✓ Show others that you are enjoying your conversation with them.

✓ Invite people to join you for dinner, social events or other activities for companionship.

✓ Let others play the expert.

✓ Get enthusiastic about other's interests.

✓ Look for the positive in those you meet.

✓ Start and end your conversation with a person's name, a handshake, and a warm greeting.

✓ Ask other people for their opinions.

✓ Let others know that you want to get to know them better.

✓ Compliment others about what they are wearing, doing or saying, but be sincere.

✓ Always search for another person's hot button.

✓ Show others that you are a good listener by restating their comments.

Smile. Don't gossip. Think positive thoughts. Believe that you're going to be remembered for being a great conversationalist — and you will be.

Communicate Like a Pro

You can network all you want, but if you don't come across as a sincere, genuine, knowledgeable and generally nice person, your networking will all be all in vain. Many times people create tension in their communication. To cut through any possible tension and to get people to like us, trust us and work with us we need to follow these guidelines for effective communication:

Don't:

✓ Accuse

✓ Make generalizations (always, never)

✓ Use labels (lazy, bad attitude, careless, unprofessional, stupid)

✓ Moralize

✓ Psychologize

✓ Assign motives

✓ Make threats

✓ Use sarcasm

Do:

✓ Say "no" in a nice way

✓ Ask questions for more information

✓ Ask questions to test your understanding of what the other has said

✓ Seek out and clarify what you have in common

✓ Focus on issues, not personalities

✓ Use "we" and "I" language

✓ Express empathy

✓ Ask for help in problem solving

Using Appointments to Move Forward

How many times do you go to a networking event only to find that you've spent the whole time just talking to one person. The problem is we don't want to rush someone or we don't want to appear rude so we just keep talking. One successful way to handle this type of scenario is to bring along your appointment book and see about meeting later.

Your conversation might go something like this, *"Joe, it's great talking to you, but I don't want to monopolize your time and you probably want to meet some more people."* At this point you might want to pull out your appointment book and say, *"I'll tell you what, I have some time available on Tuesday afternoon or Wednesday morning and I'd love to talk to you to discuss how we can work together in a mutually beneficial relationship."* If they don't have their appointment book, tell them that you will call tomorrow to either set up an appointment or confirm a time to meet.

Section

**Networking
Strategies to
Employ
AFTER the
Event**

Electronic Mail/e-mail

Electronic mail or e-mail is a must in today's high tech world. Now in a matter of seconds — a customer across the United States can be sent your price list, brochure or latest before and after photos.

Publish your e-mail address on all correspondence that leaves your office. By the turn of the century we predict that your e-mail address will be more important than your physical address.

Send e-mail to others and encourage others to send e-mail to you.

Whipping Up a Web Page

The Internet, the latest marketing tool, is available to you at little or no cost. It allows you to post your brochures, price lists, service policies, and anything else of interest. We believe the Internet is here to stay and evolve into our daily business lives.

If you can, barter your time and services to a web page designer. If you're bold you can tackle the project yourself. There are lots of web-page design software packages available.

Whichever route you choose the secret to a successful web page is whether or not it is linked. A linked page allows the user visiting other pages to visit your page with a click of his mouse. The same holds true for those visiting your page. The easiest way to get "linked" is to trade "jump-sites" with other web page holders. Pick businesses with the same demographic or psychographic profiles as you. If possible, always choose companies that are more well known than you.

The Internet is the ultimate networking environment. As video conferencing becomes more and more common, soon you may never again have to attend those 7 AM meetings away from home.

Fax Broadcast

Ever notice the trash can outside an event where hand-outs are distributed? Most of the trash consists of the hand-outs! If you want to get your message into the hands of your prospects try a broadcast fax.

Whether it's a reminder to other networkers to attend an upcoming event you are sponsoring or a weekly sales promotion for your services, fax broadcasting works.

The secret to using this valuable tool is fax software and a fax modem for your computer. You can do it on a regular fax machine, but the computer software makes it a breeze. You literally set-it and forget-it. In a matter of an hour or two you can send a few hundred faxes. If you plan on faxing more than 200 faxes, you may want to consider a true broadcast fax service. Contact your long distance carrier for more information on how to send 200+ faxes simultaneously.

Unsolicited faxes or "junk faxes" are frowned upon by most business people unless the information is useful. A few tips to consider:

✓ Keep your fax to 1 page or less. Sending multi-page "junk faxes" is a sure way to alienate prospects.

✓ Include a blurb on the fax offering to remove their name from your list of people to receive periodic faxes from you.

✓ Use a portion of the fax to educate or hold the interest of the reader. A funny cartoon or a 10 tips list works great.

✓ When you meet people always get their fax number and let them know you will send them a fax. Doing so will prevent the fax as being perceived as a "junk fax."

Fax Cover Page

Your fax cover page should be as interesting and informative as your business cards and brochures. Treat your cover page as an opportunity to sell your products or services. Include a weekly sales special, update any price changes, include your photo, use neat graphics and clip art. Don't miss out on this great opportunity to make a great impression on those you fax.

Post-Network Contact

Great networkers stay in front of the contacts they meet either in person, at regularly scheduled networking events, or by some other means available to them such as a regularly scheduled newsletter or direct mail piece. Creating and putting people on your mailing list is one way to ensure your name and information will be seen by the maximum number of your personal contacts.

The names, addresses, phone and fax numbers should be entered into a contact database. You may also want to sort your contacts by profession allowing you to send out vertical mailings to specific market segments. Other kinds of background information you may want to include: if they are currently using your product or service and if not, what competitor they are using and when does their existing commitment expire.

Landing a guest appearance on a local television, cable channel or radio show is another way to reach the masses. If you know the date and time you will appear on TV or radio, fax a little note to your contact base. You might say, *"Just a quick note to say my 15 minutes of fame has arrived. If you think of it, tune in at 6 PM tonight on channel 4, I will be on the local news."* Don't tell them too much...let them tune in and see for themselves. It's fun to know a celebrity on TV. People often point out those they personally know to others. If you land a radio spot, tape the show for posterity. Have a few copies made and send them to those who seriously wanted to hear you but missed the show.

Always take advantage of exposing yourself to the masses. It reinforces the fact that you are a mover and a shaker and that people should know and stay in touch with you.

Other ways to stay in front of the contact include:

✓ Newsletters: Send your newsletter at least four times a year. You can send it either by the traditional printed method, by e-mail, or record an audio newsletter. To make your newsletter extra special highlight your contact or include an article they wrote.

✓ Send seasonal greeting cards and gifts.

✓ Send handwritten thank you cards.

✓ Think of your network when you get extra tickets to an event or you know of something that may benefit them.

✓ Send them leads.

✓ Use their products or services.

✓ Send them articles, related to their business, especially if it's by you!

✓ Always introduce them to other people.

The bottom line is stay in touch with your contacts by helping them save, gain or accomplish something and they will always remember you.

Business Card File

Assuming that you pick up an average of 20 new business cards per networking event, it will only be a matter of time before the cards start to stack up. You should view every card as a potential sale and think of it as a commission ticket. As the years go by, eventually you will be able to trade each ticket into a cash reward.

One of the best ways to organize your business cards is with the use of an oversized Rolodex® system. The best kind is the Rolodex® RBC-600, which allows you to slip a business card into a plastic casing and file accordingly. Obtaining multiple cards from your prospects will allow you to file two cards: one under the last name of the person; and the other one under the business name of the company.

This will allow you to cross reference cards much more easily when you are searching either by company name or last name. You may even want to add a third card to your Rolodex® file under the product or service category.

For example, Joe Smith is an insurance agent who works for ABC Insurance. You may want to file one of his cards under "S" from Smith, another card under "A" for ABC Insurance and even a third card under "I" for insurance.

If you do file a third card under the business category, start from the back of the section and work forward. For example, I would file the ABC Insurance card just before the "J" section of my Rolodex® and leave the front of the "I" section available for cards that actually begin with the letter "I".

The reason to use this third card option is when you have a lead for an insurance agent and want to leverage the lead, you will have three, nine, maybe 15 insurance agents to choose from. This will also help you in your own vertical marketing efforts and the referrals you make to others. *(see Five Cards Please; Leverage Your Leads; Vertical Networking)*

Contact³ Cubed Method

Although some relationships you have now with others may have started with a sale made on the spot, most lasting relationships develop over time. If left to develop on their own, an average business relationship could take years to develop. However, using the Contact Cubed Method (Contact³), you can shorten that relationship building cycle down to as little as a few weeks.

Let's assume you meet someone for the first time at a networking event face to face and you want to further your relationship with her because they may be a prospect or power contact *(see Power Contacts)*. Here are the next steps:

✓ Follow-up with the prospect in some fashion. Because you are going to be looking for referrals from this person in the near future, you want to illustrate your professionalism and attention to detail. The best way to do that is in the form of a thank you note or a generic card note that talks about your meeting. For example, you might want to write on a generic card something like, *"It was a pleasure meeting you last week and I look forward to seeing you again at other events in the future. You mentioned that you and your firm are always on the look out for people in the X market. Although I do not personally know of anyone who is currently in the market, I do know of a person who does. I told him that you may call to pick his brain for some potential prospects. Hope this information is of help to you. Again, it was a pleasure to meet you and if I can be of service to you in anyway, please do not hesitate to call. Talk with you soon, Joe."*

✓ After you send that note, wait a week or so for some kind of a response. If you get a response then pick up the relationship from there. If you do not get a response, keep on the look out for any newspaper or magazine article related to this person's business, a hot lead, or anything else that would capture this person's attention. Once again, you will want to fax or drop a letter in the mail with the information. Wait a couple of days and then call to say hello and to confirm it has been received. Again, offer yourself as a resource and tell them to call you anytime.

Usually, by the third contact the person knows you by first name and associates a call or letter from you with good news, leads and potential business.

"When in doubt, spread it out" is a motto you should keep in mind when trying to develop relationships with others. Pacing your interactions with others rather than coming on too fast, too soon is the best way to establish strong relationships over time. One of the worst things you can do is come on too strong. Asking for too much, too soon is one way to get people to *not* want to do business with you. Also, if they feel you will act the same way with others, people will also be less likely to refer their friends and business associates to you. Remain pleasantly persistent. (*see Referrals*)

Creating an Inner Circle:
Your Own Personal Network

As you meet more and more people and attend networking event after networking event, there will reach a point where the number of events you can attend will be limited. However, just because you do not attend those events regularly, does not mean that you can't take advantage of the contacts within those groups.

Begin to create an Inner Circle or your own personal network. Identify those people who understand professional networking and the value of passing leads. Place these people in a special section in your Rolodex. This could be the fourth card. *(see Five Cards Please)*

Develop a fax network where you just send your leads to one another via fax or phone. Occasionally, you may want to call your inner circle and ask them if they have any leads for you or any expected in the near future.

Business Card Database

In addition to your Business Card File you should also create a card database on your computer. At a minimum include the obvious information such as: the person's name, title, business name, address, city, state, zip code, phone, and fax.

However, you should also include other fields such as: where you met, the date you met, a brief description of the person's business, whether or not they are or have been a customer of yours, whether or not you have ever received a lead from them, the number of leads you received from them to date, and any other additional fields common to all those in the database.

The use of a database is one of your most effective weapons in keeping in touch with all of your contacts. Even the most basic database programs will permit you to easily organize your valuable information into mailing labels, custom letters, reports, and strategic marketing information you can use for years to come.

▲

Promote Yourself Out of Non-Productive Groups

Not getting enough leads or business out of the organizations you are now affiliated with? Assuming you are using the techniques found in this book with few results, do yourself a favor and promote yourself out of the group and into another one that holds more promise. Doing this allows you to maintain the few productive relationships of the old group, and at the same time introduces you to a new community of prospects and networkers.

Small groups of people in similar professions tend to be the worst for leads. Signs that you should begin looking elsewhere include: a lack of new members, a lack of visitors or guests, spotty member attendance, and rote meetings that lack leadership and enthusiasm. Either do something dramatic to improve the group's productivity and interest level, or move on to a new group. Your time is limited and the few hours a week you have to invest in attending various networking functions is limited. Therefore you must carefully choose those events that will yield the greatest results. Do you deserve a promotion?

Follow-up, Follow-up, Follow-up

We can network all we want, but if we don't follow-up with our new found friends we will be missing opportunities to build real relationships. To build rapport, empathy and a lasting relationship, keep a database on everyone you know and create an ongoing marketing communications system. Some strategies you can follow to help you keep in touch include:

✓ Send a "just a note" letter telling the person you enjoyed meeting them.

✓ Send thank you cards and letters for purchases, referrals and ideas.

✓ Send seasonal greeting cards and gifts.

✓ Create and send out a newsletter.

✓ Send articles published by you that might be relevant to them.

✓ Call them if you have leads of people who need their services.

Saying Thanks

The best way to say thank you for a lead or a business referral is to surprise the person who sent you the lead. Whether you spend $5 or $500 on the surprise, you want it to be remembered, talked about and unexpected. Having an arsenal of gifts and gift ideas that vary in price and impact can assure that you make an impression.

As a rule of thumb, a gift for a business referral typically can range from 2 percent to 10 percent of the value of the purchase with the typical gift running in the 5 percent range. Make sure you take into consideration your profit margin and any local, state and federal laws that prohibit gifts. A good rule of thumb is that the bigger the gift the better, and I mean literally bigger is better. Why bigger? The bigger the gift, the more people will see it. The more people who see it, the more people will inquire about it, and the more people who inquire about it, the more people will hear your name.

Bigger doesn't have to be expensive. An inexpensive big gift is a bouquet of a dozen balloons delivered to the person's place of work. If you deliver the bouquet yourself, do it early before the person gets into work. Ask that it be left in the reception area rather than in their office so everyone coming to work will see it. Your total cost will be about $10 and the exposure will be tremendous. Be sure to tell the receptionist your name and why you are making the delivery. Say something like, *"Tell him the balloons are a thank you gift from Joe Smith of ABC, Inc."* Other good gifts are those that promote sharing to others in the office. In other words, if you give the person a gift and he in turn gives a little bit of the gift to those around him, then he becomes a hero at your expense. He will thank you for that with more referrals in the future. If the person works for a large company, 80+

employees, another neat gift is to have 100 carnations delivered to the office. You may want to suggest that the carnations remain in the reception area and encourage every employee to take one home as they leave for the day. To do this you might say, *"Business is blooming because of you. Thanks to you and everyone in your company for thinking of us. Please take a couple dozen of the carnations home for yourself and allow your receptionist to distribute the rest as people leave for the day. Thanks again!"*

Finally, be sure to buy any gifts from lead sources friendly to you. Buy your flowers from the florist who provides you leads. If they don't provide you leads, tell them why you are buying the flowers and say that you will do something equally as nice for them for any leads they provide to you. A thank you note is OK, but for real impact send a big thank you.

Good Conversation = Productive Networking

To become a good networker it's essential that you also become an excellent conversationalist. People will not only like you, but they will want to work with you. Use the following questions to identify characteristics of a good conversationalist:

✓ Is your voice always monotone or do you speak enthusiastically?

✓ Are you self-centered or other oriented?

✓ Do you try to dominate conversations?

✓ Do you talk too much, over explain or lecture others?

✓ Are you a complainer?

✓ Do you talk to people about their interests?

✓ Do you smile, laugh easily and respond to others genuinely?

✓ Can you discuss subjects besides your job or home life?

✓ Do you get to the point quickly or do you go into excruciating detail?

✓ Are you open, candid, direct and friendly?

✓ Do you have good eye contact?

✓ Are you an active and sympathetic listener?

✓ Do you ask others open ended questions that draw them out?

✓ Do you ask others about how they feel about a subject?

Have a Rolodex® Party

One of the best strategies for networking is to put aside about three to four hours and get together with someone else who has the types of clients and customers who would need your services — and likewise potential clients for their business.

The Rolodex® party works like this: You and the other networker get together where there are two phones. Both individuals will bring their Rolodexes® of past clients, contacts, friends, etc., and then take turns on the phone calling on behalf of the other person. This works well because if a client likes and trusts you, and you recommend the other person, that trust is transferred. Just be sure you have the confidence in the person you're recommending.

Pay Others to Market You

One of the best ways to get new business is to offer referral fees. By offering people generous incentives, you'll get plenty of business. Also, if you do get qualified referrals, make sure you pay the referrer immediately. We like to pay referrers in cash so they really get excited about finding us more work!

To make sure your referral fee program works, follow these guidelines:

✓ Pay referrers immediately. Don't make them wait, and above all, don't make them chase you down to get their referral fee.

✓ Let referrers know that if any other business comes from the client they referred, you will give them a referral fee for the next year.

✓ We give fees ranging from 10% to 20% and more. Make the incentive so great that they'll be looking for you all the time.

✓ Put the referral flyer on bulletin boards, on car windows, at events, as inserts in newsletters, and at seminars where you speak.

Here's an example of a flyer that Arnold uses to consistently generate attention and results for his speaking business!

▲

GET YOURSELF A CHECK FOR UP TO $3,000 AND MORE - - - FOR JUST A FEW MINUTES WORK!

If you know a *Meeting Planner, Training Director, Human Resources Director, Personnel Director, Association Contact or Anyone* who hires speakers and trainers ... then you have the opportunity to make big $$$$ right now!

By **referring** us to those people in your network who hire speakers and trainers **you will receive 20%** of all the money we get from our speaking or training fee. . . . Plus . . . **you will also receive 20%** of all the money we make from our product sales.

We offer customized training programs, seminars, and keynote speeches in the following areas: *Marketing and Publicity on a Low Budget, Marketing Professional Services, Exceptional Customer Service, Communicate Like a Pro, How to Make Powerful Presentations, Skills for Success, Managing Multiple Priorities, Managing and Leading People, Entrepreneurship Boot Camp and How to Become a Successful Consultant and Speaker.*

If you have one lead or many, don't miss this unique opportunity to earn big $$$ for a few minutes work!

Please feel free to contact us at:

The Business Source, Inc.
2810 Glade Vale Way, Suite 100
Vienna, Virginia 22181
703-255-3133

Become the Godfather of Referrals

The more you give the more you get. When someone gives you a lead, refers new business or an idea, make a special effort to return the favor as quickly as you can. In addition, make sure you always send a handwritten thank you to show your appreciation.

It's amazing how many people won't even thank you for a lead or an opportunity. If you really want to stand out — don't just say thanks — but find them opportunities and you'll have a friend for life. Plus the more favors you do for others the more they feel they have to do something for you.

Also always try to be ahead of the equation. So, if someone finds you an opportunity, find them two. By being the "Godfather" of referrals you'll always be the one who is owed versus being the one who owes.

Networking Hall of Fame

We want your success stories! Have a great networking story? Something you've done that works? Something you've seen others do that works? We want to know. Send your stories to the address below and you just might find your story and your name in our next book.

Mail your story to:

> Networking Stories
> P.O. Box 2583
> Woodbridge, VA 22193